Images in Black:

150 Years of Black Collectibles

Douglas
Congdon-Martin

Schiffer Publishing Ltd
1469 Morstein Road, West Chester, Pennsylvania 19380

Three cloth dolls in a wagon. *Courtesy of Fran and Jim Pohrer.*

Dedication

To Dr. Joseph Washington, prodder of consciousness and friend.

Published by Schiffer Publishing, Ltd.
1469 Morstein Road
West Chester, Pennsylvania 19380
Please write for a free catalog.
This book may be purchased from the publisher.
Please include $2.00 postage.
Try your bookstore first.

Library of Congress Catalog Number: 90-61509.

Printed in the United States of America.
ISBN: 0-88740-273-9

Acknowledgements

I am indebted to a great number of people for their help in this project. I have tried to list them all here but know that I may have missed someone.

Jan Lindenberger was of extreme assistance as she lent her expertise to the creation of the price guide, as well as sharing her collection with us and helping with the process of identification.

While I took a few of the pictures, most were taken by Tim Scott, Robert Biondi, Peter N. Schiffer, and Herbert N. Schiffer.

There would have been nothing to photograph if so many people hadn't opened their collections to us, allowing us to present this wonderful assortment of black collectibles. We thank them all for their help: Clifton Anderson; Atlantiques; Ken Aubury; Jack and Bonita Baldwin; Dee Battle; The Bookshelf; Don Boring; Maxine Caldwell; Conga Colonial; Country Classiques; Stuart Cropper; James Fitzpatrick; Don Flanagan; Pat and Rich Garthoeffner; Gemini-Hillman Antiques; Fred Giampetro; Gifted Images; John Haley; Bill Harrup, Fun Antiques; Harry and Barbara Hepbrn; Boyd Hitchner; Elizabeth Holt and Scott Lofquist; Mary Lou Holt, Holt's Country Store; House of Stuart; R.C. and Betty Hursman; Jugg Antiques; Michael Kaplan, The Tin Man; Allan Kessler; Ladybug's Cupboard; Jim Large; Jan Lindenberger, Black By Popular Demand; Jim Morrison; Gary Moss; Greg Mountcastle; N.A. Laroque & Co.; Neat Olde Things; Jacqueline Peay; Jack and Lettie Pennington; Fran and Jim Pohrer; Renata Rambarg Antiques; Milton E. Schedivy; Margaret B. Schiffer; Marianne Schneider, Schneider's Antique Toys; Seacrest Antiques; Kathleen Smith; Curtis A. Smith; Steven Still; Sweeney's Spot; Toonerville Junction; Charlene Upham; Bunny Walker; Howard and Myra Whitelaw; Frank G. Whitson.

Mary Lou Holt deserves special recognition for helping with the captions.

The staff of the Leslie Pinckney Hill Library at Cheyney University of Pennsylvania gave me the run of their wonderful collection, and helped me find what I needed.

Finally, Ellen (Sue) Taylor, as usual, has given this book its beautiful design.

I thank you all.

Douglas Congdon-Martin
West Chester, Pennsylvania

Title page photo:
Another example of Hubbell dancers from the Automatic Toy Works, circa 1875. 9.5" high. *Courtesy of Schneider's Antique Toys, Lancaster, Pennsylvania.*

Introduction

The past decade has seen a dramatic growth in the field of black collectibles and memorabilia. Once these objects were hidden away like guilty secrets. Now they are cherished and coveted by enthusiasts across the United States and abroad. They are prominently displayed by antique dealers in their shops and at shows. Increasingly black collectibles have become the center of their own exhibitions, with organizations forming to encourage the growth of the field. The desire for information has spawned many books and periodicals, including this one.

Collectors of black memorabilia come from a variety of backgrounds, and, as in any collectible field, have different reasons for their interest. It is estimated that up to seventy percent of those who collect black memorabilia are African-Americans, most of whom see how their history has been influenced by and is somehow connected to these objects. Other collectors, black and white, find the items so offensive that they purchase them simply to remove them from the marketplace. Many people simply find the items to be "cute" and receive from them a nostalgic feeling for "the good old days." Still others find that the objects reinforce their attitudes about race, allowing them to maintain the stereotypes and beliefs they have held since childhood.

Images in Black takes a broad look at the material culture that has grown out of the history of racial perceptions and misperceptions in America. It is primarily a book for collectors, but recognizes that these images have not arisen in a vacuum. They are rather part and parcel of a heritage that began in slavery and continued in racism and the fear it engendered.

Like all collectibles, black memorabilia gain added dimensions of value and meaning to the collector when they are understood in their historic and cultural context. While not pretending to be a comprehensive study, *Images in Black* tries to place these items in just such framework.

Contents

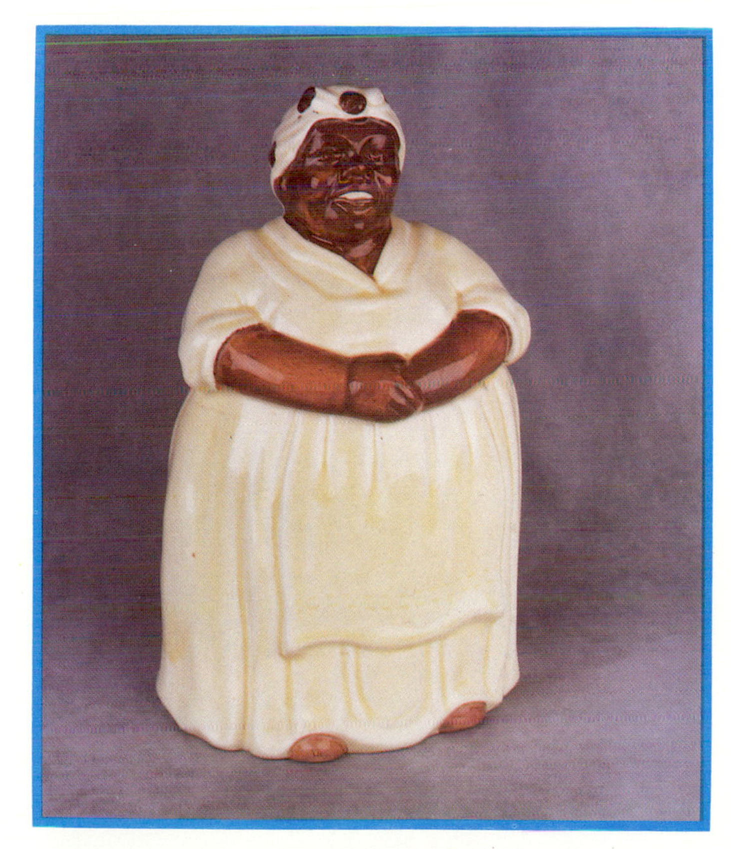

Mammy cookie jar by the Mosaic Tile Co., Zanesville, Ohio. Patented in 1944, 12.5". *Courtesy of Bunny Walker.*

Images in Black

I am an invisible man. No, I am not a spook like those who haunted Edgar Allen Poe; nor am I one of your Hollywood movie ectoplasms. I am a man of substance, of flesh and bone, fiber and liquids—and I might even be said to possess a mind. Like the bodiless heads you see sometimes in circus sideshows, it is as though I have been surrounded by mirrors of hard, distorting glass. When they approach me they see only my surroundings, themselves, or figments of their imagination—indeed, everything and anything except me.

—*Invisible Man*, Ralph Ellison

The dilemma of Ellison's *Invisible Man* has been a common experience of African-Americans through most of American history. Until the very recent past the image of black people has been largely cast by white culture. Whether in fine art, literature, drama, or the commercial arts, that image has been shaped and reshaped to meet the political, social, economic, and psychological concerns of the moment. In the process, reality and truth were sometimes sacrificed or distorted beyond recognition.

The material culture recorded in *Images in Black* traces the shaping of the image from the Civil War period through much of the twentieth century. In the toys and games, advertising, packaging, and products designed for the home, it is possible to trace the changing racial attitudes of the society. It is also clear, however, that some attitudes are deeply ingrained in the cultural consciousness and change only slowly. The roots of these attitudes can be traced to colonial America and the era of slavery.

In the seventeenth century the African-American was truly invisible. The exploration and "taming" of the new continent was of great interest in England and Europe. Artists came to the New World to record the lives and customs of the native Americans in great detail. The Indian culture had an exotic element about it that delighted the patrons of the arts and the general public alike as words and images made their way back to the Old World. The interest was so great that on several occasions Indians were brought to England so they could be seen first hand. The underlying purpose of this interaction was to increase support of the New World ventures. It was successful.

By contrast, the African is rarely seen in the artistic portrayals of the New World. The first African brought to America as a slave was with Columbus's fourth expedition in 1504. Nearly every Spanish or Portuguese exploration that followed had a contingent of African slaves (Benjamin Quarles, *The Negro in the Making of America*, p. 26). In 1619 a Dutch frigate delivered to the settlement at Jamestown, a cargo of twenty Africans who entered into indentured servanthood with the settlers. Despite this early involvement in the exploration and settlement of the Americas, Ellwood Parry, a historian, has found that, "among the colonial images...pictures of black slaves or servants in America were virtually non-existent, save for a minor figure or two in the lower corner of a decorative European map of the New World" (Ellwood Parry, *The Image of the Indian and the Black Man in American Art, 1590-1900*, p. xiii).

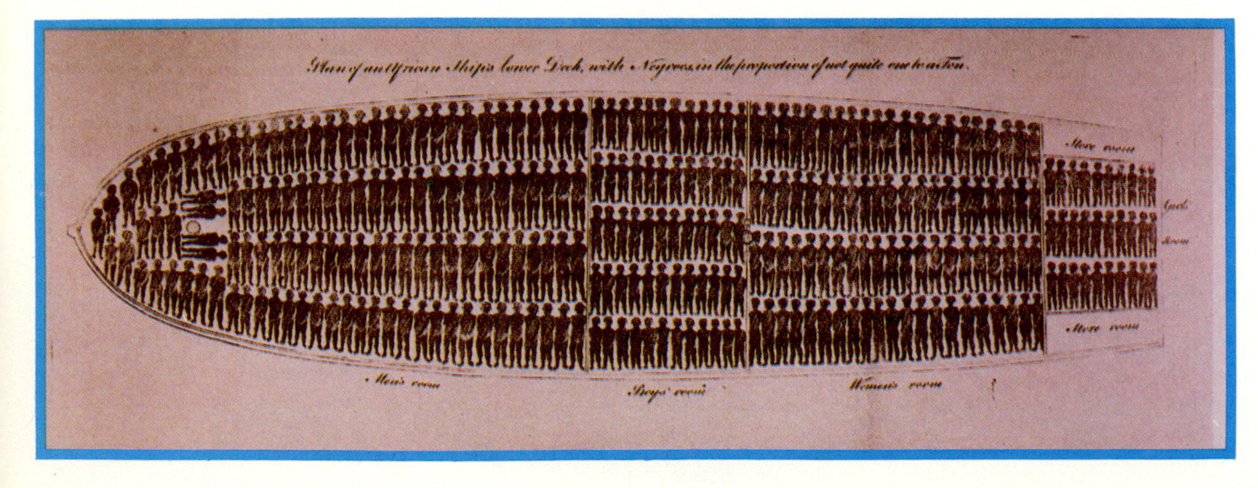

Engraving, "Plan of an African Ship's Lower Deck," 1789. American 4.25" x 3.5".

Souvenir of the Texas Centennial Exposition, 1936. Plastic figure of boy and alligator on cotton bale. 4.5″ tall. *Courtesy of Bunny Walker.*

Parry cites only a single painting during the colonial period in which a black figure has a significant role, that being one of the three kings in the *Adoration of the Magi,* by an anonymous Hudson Valley artist (Parry, pp.19 ff.). Beyond that, the appearance of African-Americans in colonial art was limited to portraits of individuals and family groupings where they were clearly servants or slaves. Almost without exception black people were placed in the background of the painting or at the feet of the white subjects of the composition, unmistakably subservient positions. Their purpose, presumably, was the same as that of the fine clothing or furnishings the artist included in the composition; they were objects which demonstrated the wealth and power of the main subjects of the portrait.

Beyond these supporting roles in colonial paintings, images of black people in colonial America are limited to the ephemera of the slave trade and its opponents. Notices of slave auctions were illustrated with crude figures of black men, women, and children, usually scantily dressed with a hint of their African origin in their costume. These notices announced new arrivals of cargos of slaves and were distributed to the plantations and communities port cities.

During and after the Revolutionary War, antislavery sentiment became organized in the form of abolitionist societies. The Pennsylvania Society was the first, formed in 1775, disbanded during the war, and revived in April, 1784. This was followed by societies in New York, New Jersey, Delaware, Maryland, Connecticut and Massachusetts. According to historian Benjamin Quarles, the "leaders of these societies could never be regarded as hot-eyed zealots," as their successors would be a half century later. "On the contrary they were men of property and standing—orderly, law-abiding, quiet-mannered" (Quarles, p. 57).

The antislavery societies met on a regular basis, organizing themselves into committees. Though their work included the basic political work of petitioning state and national legislatures, their essential strategies were more subtle. Quarles describes it as "persuasion rather than pressure, the soft impeachment rather than the denunciatory declamation" (Quarles, p. 57). Often they accomplished their aims by paying a master to free a slave. In one instance the Philadelphia society organized a boycott of goods produced by slave labor.

One tool of the "soft impeachment" was a broadside including a print of the plan and section of a slave ship, first published in England by the Committee for Affecting the Abolition of the Slave Trade, in 1787. The group, comprised primarily of Quakers, hoped that such a graphic portrayal of the inhumanity of slavery would promote its demise. A version of the print was published in America by the Philadelphia Society in 1789.

The persuasive powers of the early abolitionist societies were in themselves inadequate to ending slavery, but they did create a sentiment against the institution. Finally, on January 1, 1808, the legal slave trade from Africa was officially ended. However, the highly profitable trade continued illegally, bringing an average of 5000 smuggled Africans a year to the plantations of the southern states (Quarles, p. 64). This represented a tremendous drop in the importation of slaves. The market then shifted from importing to trading, with owners in the states of Virginia, Kentucky, and Maryland selling their surplus slaves to owners of the rapidly expanding plantations in the deep South.

SLAVE IMAGES

The images of the black person in the nineteenth century were determined by which "mirror of hard, distorting glass" reflected them. In a nation divided north and south and a century which saw much turmoil and change, the reflection was dependent upon time and place.

In the face of increasing criticism against slavery, slave owners, clergy, newspaper editors, and college professors in slave states created arguments that slavery was somehow good. They used every argument available to them, quoting scripture, political theory, and the latest wisdom of the new "science" of anthropology to shore up their position. The idea that races represented different species gained popular currency. Finding the "scientific" reasons for the superiority of one race over another became a great intellectual pursuit during the early nineteenth century, and one which the defenders of slavery used to their advantage (Thomas Gossett, *Race: The History of an Idea in America*, pp. 54 ff.). They

Very rare cast iron, hand-painted paper weight, ca. 1910. 4.25″ tall. *Courtesy of Pat and Rich Garthoeffner.*

tried to present an image to the world of "docile, tractable, and happy" slaves who were unfit for freedom (John Hope Franklin, *From Freedom to Slavery*, p. 205). One of the more widely read exponents of thisviewpoint was George Fitzhugh, an attorney from Virginia. In his book, *Cannibals All!*, written in the 1850s, he wrote:

> The negro slaves of the South are the happiest, and, in some sense, the freest people in the world. The children and the aged and infirm work not at all, and yet have all the comforts and necessaries of life provided for them. They enjoy liberty, because they are oppressed neither by care nor labor (Quarles, p. 67).

In fact slavery was among the most oppressive institutions civilization has ever devised. Its sole basis of existence was power, and the intimidation and violence power engenders. What appeared as docility or happiness, was actually a form of defense and resistance. In their 1942 study, "Day to Day Resistance to Slavery," Raymond and Alice Bauer found that African-American slaves "not only were very discontented, but they developed effective protest techniques in the form of indirect retaliation for their enslavement" (Robert V. Haynes, *Blacks in White America Before 1865*, p. 237). The resistance, sometimes conscious and sometimes the natural, unthinking response to enslavement, took several forms. Slowing up of work, inefficiency, and pretending ignorance when asked to perform a new task or use a new tool were common tactics (Quarles, p. 74).

John Hope Franklin suggested that the slaves engaged in an "elaborate program of sabotage:"

> The slave was so hard on farming tools that special ones were developed for him. He drove the animals with a cruelty that suggested revenge, and he was so ruthless in his destruction of crops that the most careful supervision was necessary to insure their survival until harvest time. He burned forests, barns, and homes to the extent that members of the patrol were frequently fearful of leaving home lest they be visited with revenge in the form of the destruction of their property by fire (Franklin, pp. 207-208).

Other forms of resistance included feigning illness, self-mutilation, and, to a lesser extent, suicide. For the more adventuresome, escape provided the answer to their oppression. Finally, and throughout the history of slavery, there were armed revolts against their owners.

Despite these obviously "unhappy" actions, defenders of slavery promoted an image of the happy slave, accepting and even grateful for his status. They were able to maintain this facade by latching onto one of the slave's means of self-preservation, what Stanley Elkins labeled the "Sambo" stereotype (Haynes, pp. 201 ff.). Quarles describes the stereotype succinctly:

> ...the slave was always playing a role, acting in the way that he believed to be to his best interests. Hence he tended to fawn servilely, to wear the mask of humility. He adopted a child posture, giving the impression of being attached to the master and utterly dependent upon him. He...pretended to be a bit stupid. This was another aspect of his technique of survival, for his apathetic gaze was self-protective; it was dangerous to know too much" (Quarles, p. 74).

The mask was effective. It hid the underlying anger and day-to-day resistance. It often allowed the slave to escape the harshest aspects of enslavement and survive. Unfortunately, the role was played so well that it was mistaken for reality. Even Elkins, writing in 1959, overlooks the evidence and suggests that "the mask had become the man" (Quarles, p. 74), an idea that has been strongly refuted by the academic community (Haynes, pp. 215 ff.).

In the early 1800s, however, the Sambo stereotype was perfectly suited to the slave owners' purposes. It allowed him to argue for the basic "goodness" of the slave system and the contented state of the slaves, while dismissing the rebellions and other resistance as scattered and insignificant anomalies. While he must have known the deeper

Chalkware ashtray with bright polychrome finish. *Courtesy of Holt's Country Store, Grandview, Missouri.*

reality behind the mask, it was seldom acknowledged or shared with the larger world. The Sambo stereotype and its variations became predominate images of the African-American throughout the nineteenth and into the twentieth centuries.

DELINEATORS & MINSTRELS

The spread and acceptance of the Sambo stereotype beyond the southern states can be traced in large part to the rise of minstrelsy as a popular form of entertainment in the nineteenth century.

Although slavery was present in the North from the earliest days, it had never been particularly important economically to the region. By 1800 the institution was in decline. Gradually African-Americans in the North were able to purchase their freedom or were liberated through the efforts of the many abolitionist societies. By 1830 slavery had virtually ceased to exist in the northern states.

Freedom was not, however, all that its advocates expected it to be. African-Americans in the North faced difficult times. With few exceptions black people were not permitted to vote. They were limited in employment to common labor or domestic service. Many who had learned a skill during slavery were unable to practice their trade when free because of white people's fear of the competition for jobs. When European immigration increased around 1840, even these menial jobs became unavailable to northern blacks.

The black population lived in poor, isolated communities. This segregation plus the small numbers of black people living in scattered communities meant that there was very little interaction between blacks and whites in the North. The black community was largely invisible to the white community, and of only minor concern. Opinions, beliefs, and stereotypes about African-Americans were not as deeply held as they were in the South.

In the early years of the nineteenth century and particularly after the War of 1812, a kind of popular nationalism took root in America. Among the general public there was a growing antipathy toward foreign things, and a desire for things American. The effects were felt at all levels of society, from government to popular culture. Newspapers, literature, and stage entertainment began to cater to this new attitude. Robert C. Toll reports that newspapers were the first to change, becoming far less formal and far more entertaining. Their stories tended to focus on the common citizen, sharing the humor, anecdotes and tall tales of the American populace. They were egalitarian to a fault, attacking anything that smacked of aristocracy or elitism (Robert C. Toll, *Blacking Up: The Minstrel Show in Nineteenth Century America*, pp. 7 ff.).

The theater was also affected by this new attitude. In urban areas of the North, theaters which had once been the bastions of the "better" classes had become a center of the community's life. While the socialites still occupied the boxes, the galleries and the pit were filled with a cross-section of the community. They were not content to sit back quietly and watch the performance. They participated, and rather boisterously at that. As Toll reports:

> In the gallery and the pit, women nursed babies, men spit tobacco juice on the floor, told jokes, cracked peanuts, ate lunches, and drank liquor. They stamped their feet in time to the music and sang along, sporadically hollering back and forth to each other. ..People got in fights, others competed with the performers, and still others somehow snored through it all (Toll, p. 11).

Despite the seeming chaos, the audience managed to pay attention to the performers. They cheered what they liked and booed what they did not, often emphasizing their displeasure by pelting the players with fruit, vegetables, stones, or other available projectiles.

It is into this culture that the minstrel emerged. While formal performances in the European style suffered greatly in this new atmosphere, the minstrel show adapted well. Toll explains:

"Minstrel Troupe," lithograph, ca. 1880. The National Printing & Engineering Co., New York. 41" x 29". *Courtesy of Titcomb's Book Shop, Sandwich, Massachusetts.*

Opposite page:
The "Banjo Player" by Jerome B. Secor, Bridgeport, Connecticut, circa 1879. Secor, originally a manufacturer of sewing machines, also developed some wonderful toys. He manufactured toys from the early 1870s until the mid-1880s, when he sold his toy business to Ives. The "Banjo Player" was featured with two other toys in *Ehrlich's Fashion Quarterly of 1879:* "Brudder Bones" and "Sister Lucinda at the Play." All are extremely rare. The "Banjo Player," clearly inspired by Minstrelsy, picks at the banjo, turns his head from side to side, moves his body, and taps his foot. *Courtesy of Schneider's Antique Toys, Lancaster, Pennsylvania.*

It was unabashedly popular in appeal, housed in its own show places, performed by middling Americans, focused on humble characters, and dominated by earthy, vital song, dance, and humor. Every part of the minstrel show—its features, form, and content—was hammered out in the interaction between performers and the vocal audiences they sought only to please. "I've got only one method," J.H. Haverly, the greatest minstrel promoter, explained, "and that is to find out what the people want and then give them that thing...There's no use trying to force the public into a theater" (Toll, p. 25).

Because of their willingness to adapt to the tastes of their audiences, the minstrel shows struck a popular chord. They catered to the growing national sentiment by presenting songs and dramas about new American heros, frontiersmen in the vein of Davy Crockett and mythical figures like Paul Bunyan. They also introduced a new American figure, the African-American, to the popular stage.

White actors had been portraying black people on stage since before the American Revolution. They had always been portrayed much as they were in other art forms of the day. They were in the background, one-dimensional figures presented for comic effect or as noble savages. In the 1820s entertainers traveled the nation performing in blackface what they described as authentic negro songs and dances. The degree of authenticity was probably less than total. The caricatures endured, but the portrayals were brought to the front of the stage and rounded out.

It is likely that the "delineators," as the white actors called themselves, did derive some of their material from contact with Southern slaves. In 1828, Thomas D. Rice, one of most popular of these "Ethiopian Delineators," observed an elderly black man doing an unusual dance while singing "Weel about and turn about and do jus so;/Every time I weel about, I jump Jim Crow" (Toll, p. 28).

He recognized the appeal this would have with audiences and added it to his show. It was a great hit, both in America and abroad. Like Rice, many of these early "delineators" traveled extensively in the South, and many of the stories, songs, and dances they included in their acts were based on the slave cultures. Sometimes two or three of them would join forces to create a song-and-dance act as a portion of a larger variety show or a circus.

The birth of the minstrel show as a complete performance happened in February, 1843 in New York City. Four black-faced delineators combined their talents to present a whole evening of the "oddities, peculiarities, eccentricities, and comicalities of the Sable Genus of Humanity" (Toll, p. 30). They called themselves the Virginia Minstrels, abandoning the more common designation of delineators. Success was immediate, and soon the country was clamoring for more. Groups formed in almost every major city of the

North, where they enjoyed long runs to enthusiastic houses. Some traveling troops headed west, following the gold rush and new settlements. A few went south, but greatest number of Minstrel troops were to be found in the Northeast.

Toll traces minstrelsy's sudden popularity first to the desire for an American entertainment, and secondly to a growing curiosity among Northerners about blacks and particularly about slavery. Unable or unwilling to see their own African-American neighbors, they accepted the minstrel performances as true representations of black people and their lives. Many performers actually believed they were seeing black performers, rather than white performers in blackface.

CHARACTERS AND STEREOTYPES FROM MINSTRELSY

The impact of the minstrel show is felt to this day. The gullibility of the audiences and the extreme popularity of the minstrel shows throughout much of the nineteenth century combined to give minstrelsy a critical role in establishing an image of blackness in the white consciousness. Most of the racial stereotypes which flourished during the past 150 years can trace their origins back to the black-faced portrayals of the minstrels. Minstrelsy was, indeed, "a hard, distorting mirror."

Guy McElroy in the introduction to *Facing History: The Black Image in American Art 1710-1940* has said "The minstrel performers...exploited the status of blacks within plantation society, reinforcing hardening perceptions of racial inequality. Minstrelsy provided a type that denied the factual details of the lives that many African-Americans led as self-sufficient individuals, providing an image that contradicted the reality much of the public experienced in both urban and rural communities."

He continues:

> ...minstrelsy relegated black people to sharply defined dehumanizing roles. Skin the color of coal, ruby lips stretched around an outsized exaggeration of a toothy grin, and the tattered clothing and mawkish behavior of such notable pioneers as T.D. Rice and Daniel Emmet created a convenient label—blacks as buffoons. Music-making, the minstrel performer's one definable skill, reduced the depth of black characterization to that of entertaining clown (Guy C. McElroy, *Facing History: The Black Image in American Art 1710-1940*, p. xiii).

While the minstrel shows displayed some ambiguity over the issue of slavery, the status of the African-American was never left to doubt. In the same show they may include the image of happy slavery inherent in the Sambo stereotype, and images of the cruelty and inhumanity of slavery. But every image, every caricature made it clear that blacks were inferior to whites. Even when the characters were sympathetic to the audience they were portrayed as "foolish, stupid, and compulsively musical" (Toll, p. 67).

Minstrels used exaggeration and creative imagination to create caricatures that would make their audiences laugh. In the process they created stereotypes that have endured for decades. They included the bulging eyes, flat, wide noses, gaping mouths, big feet that appear again and again in the objects catalogued in this book. Culturally minstrels portrayed blacks as spending an inordinate amount of time fishing or sleeping, preferring to eat possum or coon above anything else, singing and dancing through the night.

Several character types occurred over and over in minstrelsy. Free urban blacks were often portrayed as "self-centered dandies, who thought only of courting, flashy clothes, new dances, and their looks" (Toll, p. 69). While they mimicked white society, they could never quite measure up and therefore appeared the buffoon. Another caricature of the free northern black was that of the ignorant comedy type, who spoke in malaprops and had difficulty with even the simplest of ideas or inventions. In both portrayals the resulting impression was the same: the ineptitude and inferiority of the free African-American.

In scenes of plantation life that were the mainstay of minstrelsy, the principal characters were made in the Sambo image. They were portrayed as happy slaves, and although they sometimes tricked or ridiculed their masters, the minstrel blacks usually praised them for their kindness and generosity. The plantation was presented as the setting for a great happy extended family, including both slave and master.

Romance on the plantation was highly valued in these portrayals and usually involved another caricature: the alluring "yaller gal." Of light skin and white facial features, she was described as beautiful and highly desirable. She alone seemed above ridicule, her roles usually involving "coquettish flirtations, happy romances, and sad, untimely deaths" (Toll, p. 76). Toll points out that while this sensual figure was an important part of minstrel shows, the male characters were never portrayed as sexually attractive.

Indeed, the only attractive male stereotype in minstrelsy was the asexual "Old Darky." Toll describes these characters as "white-haired 'Old Uncles'... [They] possessed what nineteenth-century Americans considered the sentimental qualities of 'heart' without the balancing qualities of the 'mind'" (Toll, pp. 77 ff.). He was the common man, possessed of emotion, able to laugh, to love, and to cry, even if he could not think.

"Old Uncle's" female counterpart in the minstrel cast of characters was the Mammy or "Old Auntie." She was the well-loved matriarch, the glue that held the family together. A song from one of the minstrel routines describes her well (New Orleans Serenaders, "Aunt Dinah Row," in Toll, p. 79):

> She'd joke wid de old folks and play wid de child
> She'd cry wid de sorrowing, laugh wid de gay;
> Tend on de sick bed, and join in de play
> De fust at de funeral, wedding, or birth
> De killer ob trouble and maker ob mirth
> She spoke her mind freely, was plain as de day
> But never hurt any by what she might say.
> If she once made a promise, it neber was broke.

The effect of Darky Uncle and Aunt upon the audience was to offer white America "openness, warmth, devotion, and love. The romanticized plantation served as a sanctuary where they and the natural family ties they epitomized had a chance to develop and mature, immune from the forces of 'progress'" (Toll, p. 27). The power and the endurance of the image is clear in the pages that follow. Whether as Aunt Jemima, Uncle Ben, or any number of variations on the theme, the stereotypes have continued their appeal to the present day.

Black minstrel troupes began to appear in the mid-1850s in major American cities. After the Civil War, as white minstrelsy began to fade, black

Sheet music cover for the music of J.M. Busby's Colored Minstrels, featuring the stars of the show. Left, Effie Moore, "The Black Melba;" center, the Harrison Bros. Minstrels; right, Mr. Boyd (?). Published by Will Rossiter, Chicago. *Courtesy of Elizabeth Holt and Scott Lofquist.*

shows gained in popularity. They claimed to bring a new authenticity, many of the performers being "former slaves," and they certainly brought some new energy to the form. The form, content, and character of black minstrel shows differed very little from their white predecessors. White audiences, though drawn to the novelty of black minstrels, still expected to see the same images, the same stereotypes the white troupes had created.

Interestingly, despite its strong satire and negative caricature, black minstrelsy also appealed to black audiences. Toll suggests that this popularity can be traced to the common experience shared by the audience and the performer. Unlike the black-faced white minstrel, the black minstrel could be "trusted." He knew the truth about life in America for black people. "When blacks 'from the mass' heard him, then, they heard their own dialect, their own slang, their own jokes: in short, their own culture. They did not worry what whites thought of it. Feeling a common bond with the performer, they laughed and cheered" (Toll, p. 258).

Black minstrelsy was popular through the 1890s, though its appeal faded in the early twentieth century. It was the training ground and the beginning of a strong tradition of black entertainers.

It is difficult to overestimate the impact of minstrelsy, both black and white, for it was a predominate entertainment form for at least sixty

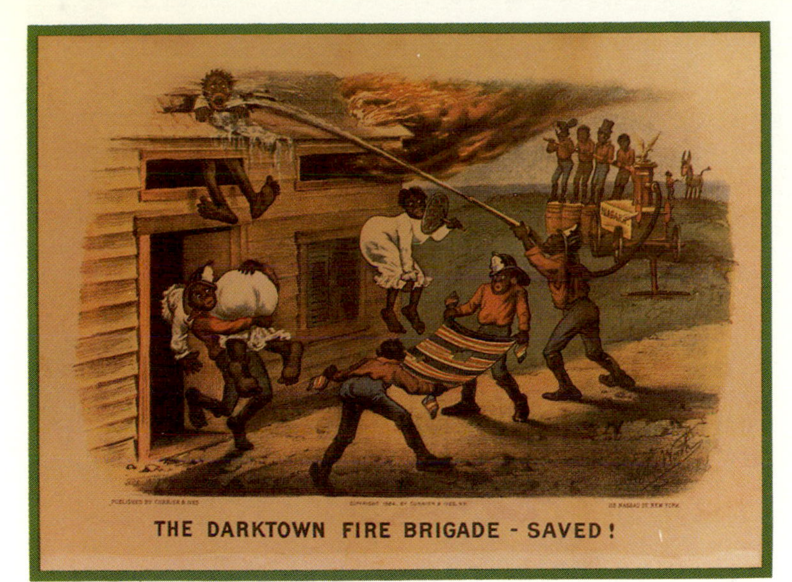
THE DARKTOWN FIRE BRIGADE - SAVED!

"The Darktown Fire Brigade—Saved!" Lithograph by Thomas Worth, copyright 1884 by Currier & Ives, New York.

years. It was seen by millions of people over that period, many of whom believed that what they were seeing was a factual portrayal of the lives of African-Americans, both slave and free.

The immediate effect according to McElroy, was that minstrelsy

> provided a type that denied the factual details of the lives that many African-Americans led as self-sufficient individuals, providing an image that contradicted the reality much of the public experienced in both urban and rural communities...These characters...objectified the distinctive individuality of African-American communities...This lack of individuality could, in turn, be used to justify the maintenance of an economy supported to a large extent by the labor of an indentured rural black underclass" (McElroy, p. xiii).

The long-term, indirect impact of the stereotypes and images created in minstrelsy comes from their broad, and enduring acceptance in popular culture. From newspapers of the nineteenth century to television shows of the twentieth, the images recur in forms that are only slightly altered from minstrel days. Children's toys of the nineteenth and early twentieth centuries were often taken directly from minstrelsy, as were the images that became popular in advertising and packaging. Figures and trinkets that have adorned many American kitchens in the twentieth century recall the minstrel "Uncle" and "Auntie" in molded plastic or ceramic. For many people, these images comprise their understanding of black people. It is an understanding based in a comic interpretation that is one hundred fifty years old. It is, in fact, a misunderstanding.

OTHER IMAGES

Two other stereotypes deserve at least brief mention in the interest of completeness, though they have little representation in the collectibles included in this volume. The first is that of the sexually aggressive black male. Following the Civil War, the years of reconstruction offered a short period of relative social equality and political enfranchisement of black people in America. Throughout the South black people were elected to office and took over the leadership of many business, social, and political institutions.

The trend caused a great deal of resistance among members of the white communities in both the South and the North who used the stereotypes created in the minstrel shows to lampoon the black leaders as dandies and buffoons. A new stereotype also emerged: that of the black man who aggressively sought sexual relations with white women.

While it is impossible to accurately trace the source of this new stereotype, its spread can be attributed to the influence of the Ku Klux Klan and similar groups formed to resist Reconstruction. The "threat to white womanhood" was a central element of their cause and the phobic fires they fanned to build support. They were successful. Aggressive attacks by conservatives in the South and apathetic responses by Republicans in the North led to the abandonment of Reconstruction in 1877 when federal troops were withdrawn. Jim Crow laws were rapidly adopted, insuring the separation of the races and disenfranchisement of blacks.

The threat of rape that black men supposedly presented to white women, was used to explain and justify the horror of lynching as an instrument of justice. In fact, of the 3811 lynchings of black men between 1889 and 1941, only 641, or 17%, were even accused of rape, either attempted or committed. Gossett reports that "Negroes were lynched for such 'crimes' as threatening to sue a white man, attempting to register to vote, enticing a white man's servant to leave his job, engaging in labor union activities, 'being disrespectful' or 'disputing with' a white man, or sometimes for no discoverable reason at all" (Gossett, p. 269).

The stereotype, more powerful than the fact, was exploited in the novels and other writings of the time. Thomas Dixon Jr.'s *The Clansman* written in 1905 is a story of Reconstruction which reflected a violent hatred of Negroes. It included this description of a black rapist:

> "He had the short heavy-set neck of the lower order of animals. His skin was coal black, his lips so thick that they curled both ways up and down with crooked blood-marks across them. His nose

Sign for segregated restrooms, marked "L & N." *Courtesy of Holt's Country Store, Grandview, Missouri.*

was flat and his enormous nostrils seemed in perpetual dilation. The sinister bead eyes, with brown splotches in their whites, were set wide apart and gleamed ape-like under his scant brows. His enormous cheekbones and jaws seemed to protrude beyond the ears and almost hide them."

The Clansman became a popular novel, and its influence on racial attitudes was great. Greater still, however, was its movie version, *The Birth of A Nation*, produced by D.W. Griffith in 1915. In the early days of motion pictures this film was a technical and dramatic triumph. Highly praised, it was seen by millions of Americans who absorbed a graphic portrayal of all the worst stereotypes of black people. They saw images of southern blacks during Reconstruction rigging elections and keeping white voters from the polls by force. They saw black legislators, with bare feet propped on their desks and whisky flasks in their hands, passing laws which permitted intermarriage. And in the climax of the film, they saw a renegade black man chasing a young white girl through the woods. To avoid rape she killed herself by leaping from a high rock. Her brother, seeking to avenge her death, formed a mob that lynched the black man, and then organized a unit of the Ku Klux Klan to reestablish the authority and dominance of white men (Gossett, p. 340).

More than minstrelsy, more than novels, the motion picture had the power to convince viewers of the truth and reality of what they saw. It is probably not coincidental that 1915 also saw the rebirth of the Ku Klux Klan, which had been dormant. The stereotype of the dangerous black male had established itself in the white cultural consciousness, where it still can be found.

Finally there is the stereotype of the black person as an athlete. This is a positive image and one that is highly important to the black community. One of its earliest expressions was in the Dark Town Battery cast iron mechanical banks in the 1880s. Pamela Nelson comments on the bank saying, "racial segregation in baseball was not as complete as it would become by the start of the twentieth century, and it apparently was acceptable for a short period to depict positive images of blacks as athletes" (Pamela Nelson, *Ethnic Images in Toys and Games*, p. 13). Except for an occasional boxer, like Joe Lewis, or olympic hero, like Jesse Owens, these images would largely disappear until the last half of the twentieth century when Jackie Robinson broke the color line and entered major league baseball. Gradually, as shown initially on baseball cards and continuing with toys and advertising, the black athlete has become an accepted and cherished image.

Unfortunately, as with all stereotypes, this image tends to focus on one aspect of the person while ignoring others. The detrimental effect of this is easily seen when one looks at the number of college athletes who graduate without the skills they need to lead productive lives. Colleges are guilty of exploiting athletic skill and at the expense of intellectual development. If these school athletes are not among the elite few who qualify to become professional athletes they may begin their adult lives with a severe, and usually permanent, handicap.

When Ralph Ellison wrote *Invisible Man* at the end of the 1940s the image of the African-American was about to undergo a dramatic and far reaching change, but it did not happen all at once. Two world wars, migration from southern rural farms to the northern industrial cities, highly visible black educational, scientific, political, and artistic leaders, a cultural renaissance in the 1920s—all these influences and Ellison's own work had contributed to the change. The "mirrors of hard, distorting glass" were beginning to crack. Stereotypes, which caused a "peculiar disposition of the eyes of those with whom I come in contact" causing them to see "only my surroundings, themselves, or figments of their imaginations," began to loosen their hold on minds and hearts of the nation.

The years that have followed have seen new images emerge, images of leadership, of a people struggling to be free, of success, beauty, and intelligence. It would nice to think that the old stereotypes and attitudes have passed away, but they have not. They are deeply ingrained in the American culture. Perhaps, though, by facing them directly and seeking to understand them, we can remove them from our field of vision and begin to see one another as we really are.

Part One: Childhood Things

Mechanical Toys

No part of material culture is quite as insightful as the things of childhood. Toys, games, and dolls are reflections of the ethics, customs, fears, and beliefs of a society. They create a miniature world where children can learn the ways of the larger world. By mimicking the actions of their elders children use toys to discover how things work, how people relate, and how they can have an impact upon their surroundings.

Before the Industrial Age brought mass-produced toys, most were handmade. Some were as simple as a stick transformed by the miracle of imagination into a sword or a gun. Others, though made by untrained hands, revealed the skills and the artistry of their creators. These folk toys have a particular beauty, simple, colorful, and full of life.

The favorite form of black folk toy was the doll. By giving a human form to a little piece of fabric and filling it with straw or stuffing, the maker imbued it with life. The earliest of these black cloth dolls were made primarily for the play of black children. While their features were less than realistic, they generally were not blatantly offensive. Like white folk dolls, they had a primitive beauty that endeared them to the child who played with them then, as it does to the collectors who cherish them today.

With the growth of the industrial age manufactured dolls entered the marketplace. They included the "Topsy-Turvy" doll which had a black face and a white face and could be turned either way. Usually, but not always, the black side of the doll would be dressed as a servant and the white side dressed as a mistress.

Most of the early manufactured dolls stuck to accepted stereotypes of exaggerated characteristics or roles. Over the years, however, the stereotypes softened somewhat, and in the twentieth century realistic black dolls became available from some manufacturers. A German-made doll, the "Bye-Lo Baby," was introduced in the United States in early 1920s. Despite fears that it was too realistic, it became a top-seller (Nelson, 9. 17). While the number of ethnic dolls has never been great, there has been a growing commitment since then to create realistic dolls.

The industrial age also brought other toys to the market place. Ives and other great manufacturers

"The Five Jolly Darkies" wooden mechanical toy from the Civil War era. W.S. Reed Toy Company, Leominster, Massachusetts. 9" x 6.5". *Courtesy of Allan Kessler, Chicago.*

Mechanical pull toy of metal, composition, and fabric. As the toy is pulled the bell is rung. New York Toy/American Toy Co., ca. 1860. 5.5" x 6". *Courtesy of Toonerville Junction, Allentown, Pennsylvania.*

Automaton picture. When activated the devil peers through the window and bursts in the door. The sleeping man wakes and sits upright in bed. 11.25" x 14.75" x 4.5". *Courtesy of Margaret B. Schiffer.*

Wooden dancing figure, made to move by tapping the stick to the rhythm of the music. Still a popular folk toy, this one probably dates to the last quarter of the 19th century. *Courtesy of Fran and Jim Pohrer.*

A very early mechanical toy, it is weight driven to rock the cradle with the white baby while the mammy looks on. Manufactured by the New York Toy Co. in the 1860s, it was distributed by Ives. *Courtesy of Toonerville Junction, Allentown, Pennsylvania.*

Juba Dancers, patented as Automatic Toy Dancers by William L. Hubbell on February 17, 1874. Manufactured circa 1874 by Automatic Toy Works, which was started as American Mechanical Toy Co., and later bought by Ives. *Courtesy of Hillman-Gemini Antiques, New York.*

of clockwork toys used black figures in many of their toys. Many of these mechanical figures were taken directly from the minstrel shows that enjoyed such great popularity during the mid-nineteenth century. "Juba Dancers," "Mr. Bones," "The Stump Speaker," and many others were from popular minstrel roles and routines. Like minstrelsy itself, they had an appeal to both white and black children, an appeal enhanced by their fine construction.

A more disturbing trend in early manufactured toys was the portrayal of African-Americans as objects of violence. Typical of these toys is the mechanical bank "Always Did 'Spise a Mule." It depicts a black person who is thrown from the mule he is riding when a coin was placed in his mouth. Nelson suggests that this involves the player "in pretend violence against an African American and [implies] that such violence is fun. (Nelson, p.11)

The little girl dances as the finely dressed man plays the bell. Maker unknown, circa 1870-80. 8.5" x 9". *Courtesy of Schneider's Antique Toys, Lancaster, Pennsylvania.*

"Old Black Joe" by Ives, circa 1876. Walking figures were patented by Arthur Hotchkiss of Cheshire, Connecticut in 1875. He sold the rights to Ives, which introduced several figures over the following years. The clockwork mechanism was in the body and moved the legs back and forth. The cast iron feet had wooden rollers, which can be seen in this example. The heads and hands are cast metal with two halves joined together to create a hollow center. 10" tall. *Courtesy of Schneider's Antique Toys, Lancaster, Pennsylvania.*

"The Preacher" by Ives, circa 1875. This figure bends at the waist, moves its hand and head. It is similar to the "Woman's Rights Advocate" from Clay's Automatic Toy Works, and the "Political Stump Speaker" first manufactured by Clay and later by Ives. 10" tall. *Courtesy of Schneider's Antique Toys, Lancaster, Pennsylvania.*

The same trend can be seen in the popular manufactured games. Coming at end of the nineteenth century, a time when blacks were encountering growing hostility in the nation, a recurring theme of these games involved violence toward black people. "The Jolly Darkie Target Game" and "Hit the Dodger! Knock Him Out!" were two of many games that involved throwing objects at black figures. The theme also was carried into board games like "The Funny Game of Hit or Miss" whose board included faces of the black men, which the player either "hit" or "missed" depending on the spin of the top. Even a toy as innocent as jigsaw puzzle was given the provocative name, "Chopped Up Nigger."

Before the mid-1950s it was rare to find a toy that did not involve exaggeration, stereotype, or violence against a black person. Nelson cites the "Darktown Battery" mechanical bank as one of the few positive representations of black people in toys. Many dolls and a few other toys can also be counted as being neutral or positive. But the real change came with the civil rights movement. As concern for the place of toys in the development of a child's attitudes grew and companies began to realize the largely untapped market of the African-American consumer, more realistic images began to appear in toys. Positive roles were created, black heros were portrayed, and glamour dolls and dolls with realistic features began to be manufactured with dark skin.

If toys are reflective of society, then perhaps there is reason to believe that we have made some strides in racial tolerance and understanding.

"Brudder Bones" by Jerome B. Secor, Bridgeport, Connecticut, circa 1879. Also inspired by the Minstrel shows of the 19th century, "Brudder Bones" shakes the bones in both hands, sways and moves his head. *Courtesy of Schneider's Antique Toys, Lancaster, Pennsylvania.*

"Tomb Alabama Coon Jigger." Similar to Lehmann's EPL 685 and 690. Possibly licensed or "borrowed." 9.75" x 5.5". *Courtesy of Country Classiques.*

"Oh-My Alabama Coon Jigger" tin toy by E.P. Lehmann. Made in models EPL 685 and 690, this wind-up toy was manufactured from 1911 to 1945. A similar tap-dancing figure was first patented by Walter S. Hendren of Nicholasville, Kentucky in 1910 and registered in Germany in 1911. It is unclear how Lehmann got around this patent, but he brought his ingenuity and marketing skill to the toy. 9.75" x 5.5". *Courtesy of the collection of The Tin Man, Michael Kaplan.*

Tin wind-up toy porter, ca. 1925. Similar to Lehmann's popular "Tap Tap," EPL 560, this was possibly made by Girard. 6" tall. *Courtesy of Pat and Rich Garthoeffner.*

"Zig Zag" manufactured by Lehmann, ca. 1907. The black and white figure supported between two large wheels (one missing). Tin with a wind-up mechanism, 5" tall. *Courtesy of Howard and Myra Whitelaw.*

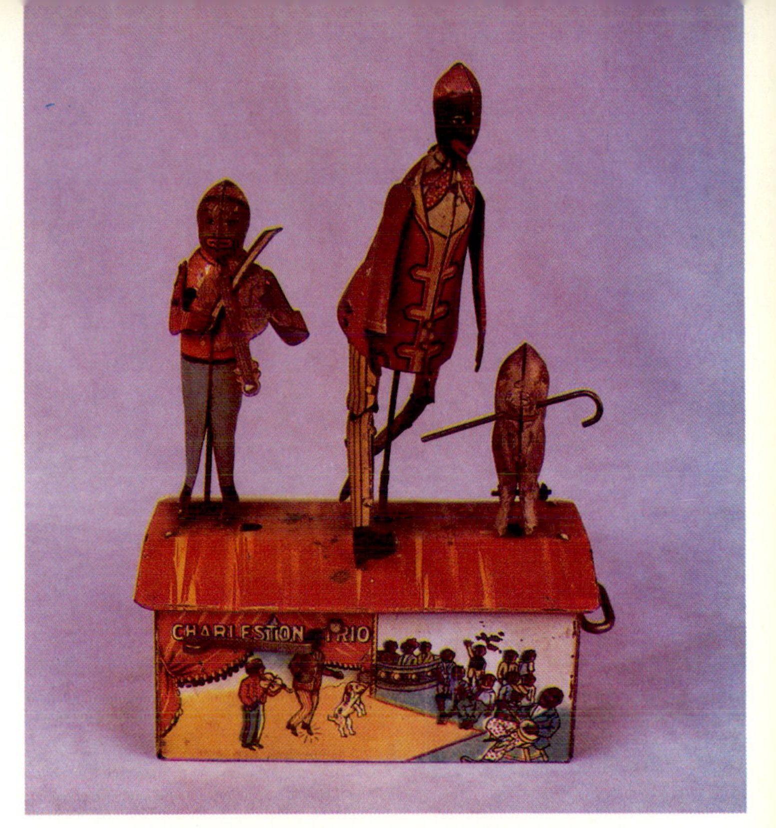

"Charleston Trio" by Louis Marx, ca. 1921. Lithographed tin with wind-up mechanism. 8.5" x 4.5". *Courtesy of Bunny Walker.*

This musical couple is from Germany, ca. 1910. Made of tin, they circle and spin to the music. 9.5" tall. *Courtesy of Hillman-Gemini Antiques, New York.*

"Ham and Sam the Minstrel Team" is a mechanical tin toy patented by Samuel Berger, of Newark, New Jersey in 1924. *Courtesy of a private collection.*

"Jazzbo-Jim, The Dancer on the Roof" was patented by Samuel Berger in 1921. First manufactured by Strauss, it was later made by Louis Marx Company. The toy danced and played the banjo when wound up. *Courtesy of Fran and Jim Pohrer.*

"Knock Out Prize Fighters" was manufactured by the Ferdinand Strauss Company of New York in ca. 1924. *Courtesy of Tony and Nancy Sabestinas, Collectible Hobby House, Kearney, New Jersey.*

This variation of "Jazzbo-Jim" has a fiddler to accompany the dancer, circa 1925. Identical figures are known to have been used on the "Charleston Trio" toy by Louis Marx. The same toy with somewhat different figures was made by Line Mar Toys, a subsidiary of Louis Marx around 1953. *Courtesy of Fran and Jim Pohrer.*

A rare nicely formed wind-up figure, probably German. Celluloid, 5.5". *Courtesy of a private collection.*

"Amos 'n' Andy" taxi cab manufactured by Louis Marx, New York, in the 1930s. The popular radio show generated several product spin-offs. 5" x 8". *Courtesy of Holt's Country Store, Grandview, Missouri.*

The skating waiter is of tin and has a windup mechanism. Manufacturer unknown. *Courtesy of Holt's Country Store, Grandview, Missouri.*

"Pango Pango African Dancer" manufactured by T.P.S., Japan, ca. 1950s. Lithographed tin, 6" tall. *Courtesy of The Bookshelf.*

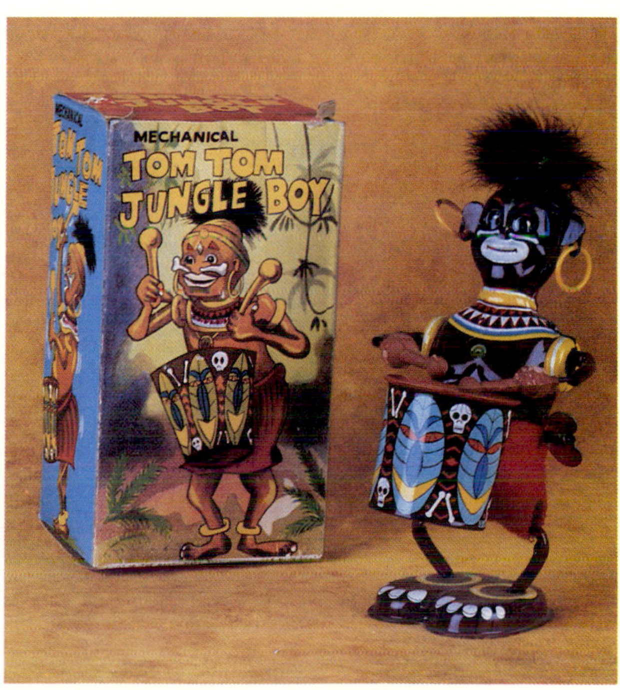

"Tom Tom Jungle Boy" manufactured in Japan, ca. 1950s. Lithographed tin, 7" tall. *Courtesy of The Bookshelf.*

Brightly colored wooden toy geared so the mule's legs move when it is pushed or pulled. Ca. 1930s. *Courtesy of Bunny Walker.*

"The Smallest Boxer in the World" is a wooden finger toy manufactured in Germany, ca. 1930. *Courtesy of a private collection.*

The clown and the dandy are finger puppets, similar to the example above. *Courtesy of Fran and Jim Pohrer.*

Amos 'n' Andy sparkler of German manufacture, ca. 1930. *Courtesy of Allan Kessler, Chicago.*

Lithographed tin spinning noisemaker, 4.5" tall. *Courtesy of Frank G. Whitson, Baltimore, Maryland.*

These wooden stick figures were mounted on the arm of a phonograph and would dance with the vibration of the machine. Probably manufactured by the National Company, Boston, ca. 1910-1915, 6" tall. *Courtesy of Allan Kessler, Chicago.*

Talking Machine Toys, circa 1915, National Company, Boston. The boxers are identical to the boxers in the "Knock Out Prize Fighters" toy by Strauss Company shown elsewhere in this section. *Courtesy of Hillman-Gemini Antiques, New York,*

Trade stimulator with a moving head, 16″ high. *Courtesy of Jan Lindenberger, Black By Popular Demand, Colorado Springs, Colorado.*

Trade stimulator, German, 1890-1900. The head goes from side to side and the cigarette moves in the opposite direction. Original clothes, 23″ high. *Courtesy of Stuart Cropper, Sussex, England.*

Dolls

Two rag dolls with painted eyes and faces. *Courtesy of N.A. Laroque & Co.*

Rag doll with yarn hair and button eyes. *Courtesy of Fred Giampetro.*

Cloth and straw rag doll. *Courtesy of Conga Colonial.*

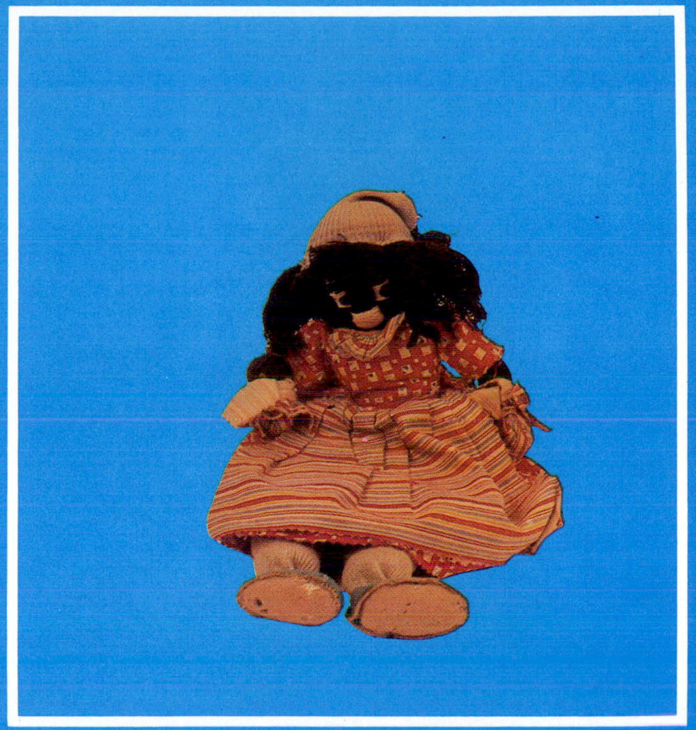

Gaily dressed yarn doll. *Courtesy of Fran and Jim Pohrer.*

Colorfully dressed rag doll of similar design to the previous example. *Courtesy of Jacqueline Peay.*

15″ rag doll. *Courtesy of a private collection.*

24″ rag doll with painted eyes and mouth, and a colorful costume. *Courtesy of Holt's Country Store, Grandview, Missouri.*

Nicely made rag doll with button eyes and cloth hair done in braids. *Courtesy of Fran and Jim Pohrer.*

Award-winning cloth dolls. *Courtesy of Fran and Jim Pohrer.*

Clothed mammy doll bottle with button eyes, shaped nose and embroidered features. *Courtesy of Fran and Jim Pohrer.*

Cloth doll with shaped nose and embroidered facial features. *Courtesy of Elizabeth Holt and Scott Lofquist.*

Two nicely dressed rag dolls. *Courtesy of Fran and Jim Pohrer.*

Two mammy-styled cloth dolls. The doll on the left has painted features and the one on the right is embroidered with button eyes. *Courtesy of Holt's Country Store, Grandview, Missouri.*

Cloth minstrel doll with applied felt lips, button eyes, and a straw hat. *Courtesy of Fran and Jim Pohrer.*

Cloth black face pillow in the Raggedy Ann style.
Courtesy of Holt's Country Store, Grandview, Missouri.

Cloth mammy doll. *Courtesy of Betty and R.C. Hursman.*

A pair of rag dolls with painted eyes and mouths and other embroidered features. *Courtesy of Fran and Jim Pohrer.*

Cloth mammy doll with inset face made of charcoal. 3" tall. *Courtesy of Fran and Jim Pohrer.*

Small cloth doll with a hint of where its facial features once were. *Courtesy of Fran and Jim Pohrer.*

Yarn doll, Norma DeCamp, North Carolina, 1989. *Courtesy of Wizard's Work, Cape May, New Jersey.*

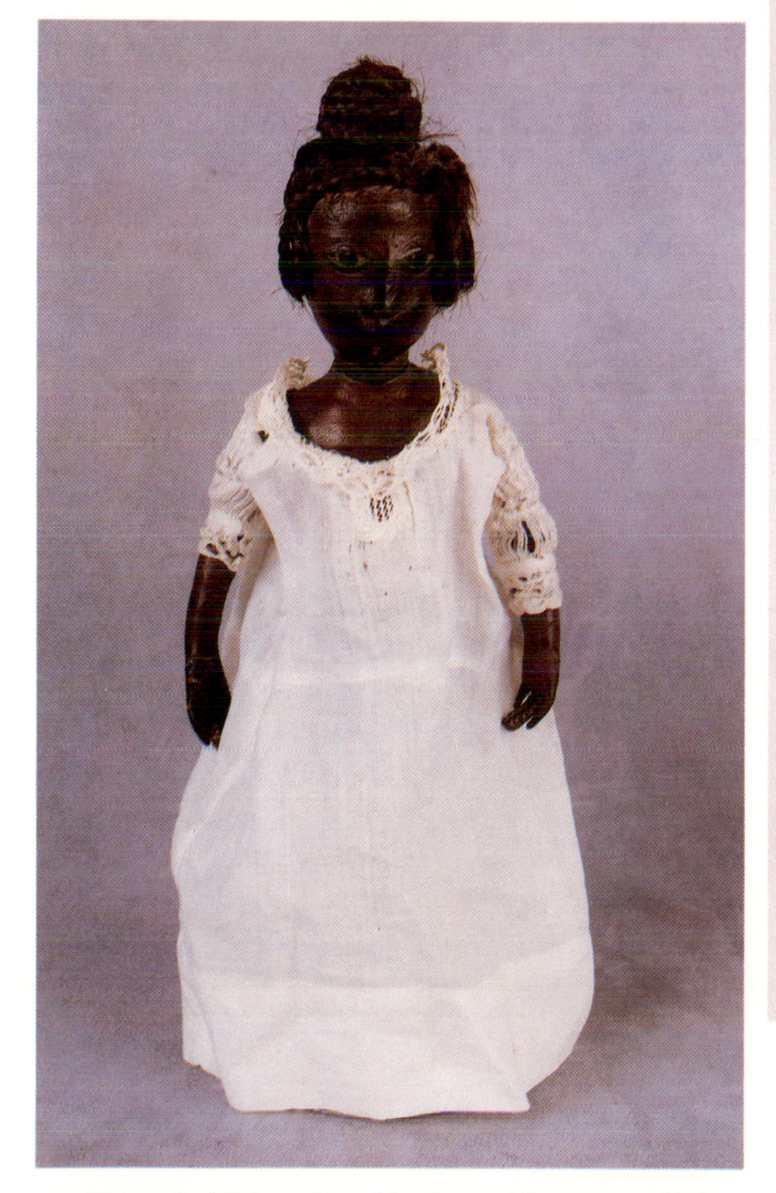

This soft doll has skin of leather, with nicely molded features and real hair. *Courtesy of Charlene Upham.*

Female rag doll with finely molded head and facial features of fabric. The fingernails are made of quill. *Courtesy of Fran and Jim Pohrer.*

Topsy-turvy doll featuring a blue-eyed white girl in a pristine white dress and a black servant girl. Lithographed cloth. *Courtesy of Fran and Jim Pohrer.*

Painted papier mâché heads and arms are attached to the cloth body of this topsy-turvy doll. 9.5″ tall. *Courtesy of a private collection.*

Topsy-Turvy

Celluloid topsy-turvy doll. *Courtesy of Betty and R.C. Hursman.*

A variation on the topsy-turvy doll is this cloth two-faced doll. *Courtesy of Fran and Jim Pohrer.*

These two ladies with their embroidered features are equally, and elegantly, adorned. *Courtesy of Fran and Jim Pohrer.*

This cloth topsy-turvy doll dates from the Civil War era and has its original costuming. The facial features are painted. *Courtesy of a private collection.*

A lithographed cloth topsy-turvy doll from the late 19th century. *Courtesy of a private collection.*

A lithographed cloth topsy-turvy doll in a fine brocade. Late 1900s. *Courtesy of a private collection.*

Stuffed Dolls

Full-color, ready-to-sew dolls have been popular since the late nineteenth century. Davis Mills, and later Quaker Oats, often used them as premiums for their Aunt Jemima line, and dry goods stores carried them for sale. *Courtesy of Holt's Country Store, Grandview, Missouri.*

A typical mammy doll available in retail stores. The fabric includes one large doll and one small one. Finished examples can be seen in the preceding group photo at the back right and front left. Copyright 1910 by Saalfield Publishing Co., Akron, Ohio. *Courtesy of a private collection.*

On the left is a completed "Pickaninny" doll from the Arnold Print Works pattern. The doll on the right is made of papier mâché, with molded features. 15" high. *Courtesy of a private collection.*

"Pickaninny" doll. Patented July 5, 1892 by the Arnold Print Works, North Adams, Massachusetts. *Courtesy of Kathleen Smith.*

The Aunt Jemima doll was offered as a premium many different times from 1905 to the late 1940s. With each offering the dolls changed in form and appearance as the logo developed within the company. This doll probably dates to the 1916 promotion. *Courtesy of a private collection.*

In 1917 Davis Mills introduced a more natural representation of Aunt Jemima. These dolls are from the period of 1917-1929. From left to right they are: Diana, "Aunt Jemima's little girl;" Uncle Mose, "Aunt Jemima's husband;" Aunt Jemima; and Wade, "Aunt Jemima's little boy." The adults are 15" tall, the children 12". *Courtesy of Jan Lindenberger, Black By Popular Demand, Colorado Springs, Colorado.*

A 1929 pattern for an Uncle Mose doll. The Quaker Oats Company, St. Joseph, Missouri. *Courtesy of a private collection.*

The completed 1929 Uncle Mose doll. *Courtesy of a private collection.*

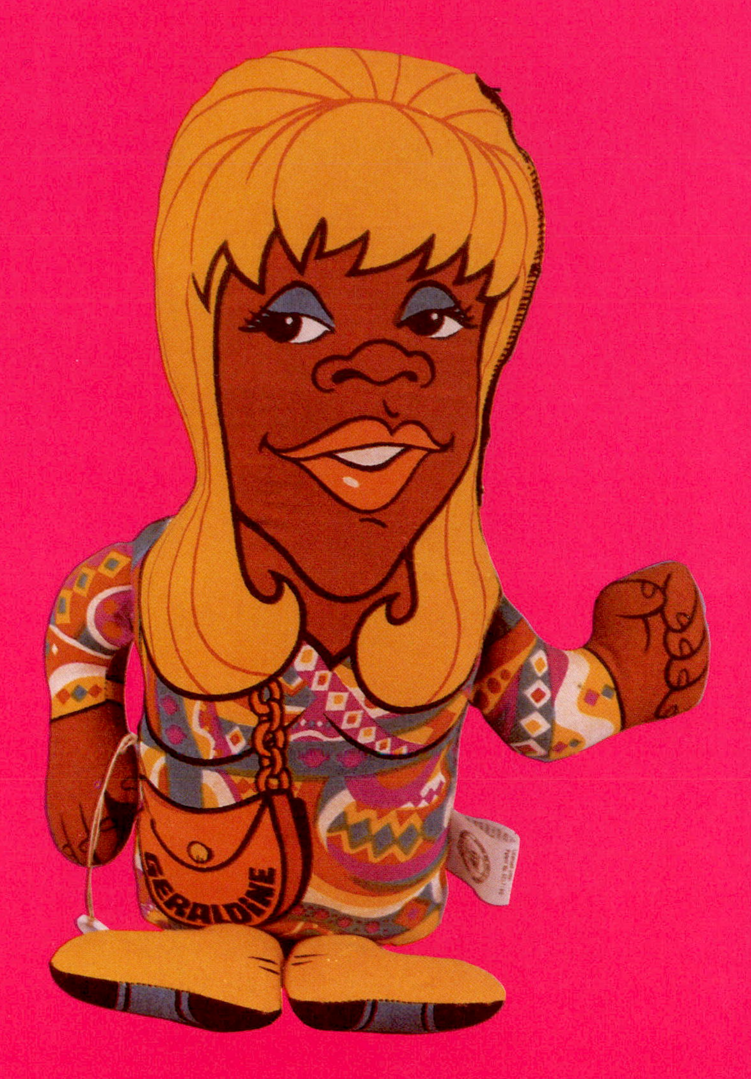

The comedian Flip Wilson was at the height of his popularity in the late 1960s and early 1970s. These stuffed talking dolls of Flip and his female character, Geraldine, are by Streetcorner Productions Inc., 1970. They were made in Taiwan. *Courtesy of Holt's Country Store, Grandview, Missouri.*

A 1949 Raggedy Ann-styled Aunt Jemima doll. 12″ tall. *Courtesy of Jan Lindenberger, Black By Popular Demand, Colorado Springs, Colorado.*

Shoulder plate doll, with glass eyes. Cloth body and painted papier mâché head, arms, and feet. The doll squeaked when its middle was squeezed. 13" tall. Circa 1880-1890. *Courtesy of a private collection.*

"Tom" by Leo Moss, 1931. "Tom" is made of papier mâché with a soft, commercially made body and glass eyes. Leo Moss was the son of slaves who lived in Macon, Georgia. He made dolls that featured family and friends. After 1930 his dolls all have tears. The story, perhaps apocryphal, is that the tears started after Moss's wife ran away with a white doll dealer. This piece was found in Gainesboro, Georgia in a state of neglect. It has the gray-green color of authentic Moss dolls. Fakes have been made and are generally browner in color. 17" tall. *Courtesy of Greg Mountcastle, Atlanta, Georgia.*

Composition Dolls

Wood and composition doll finely attired in a purple coat. The Shoenhut Toy Company, ca. 1920. 9" tall. *Courtesy of Curtis A. Smith.*

"Sadie" is a contemporary black doll made in 1989, by Mrs. Crinkleton of Chile, North Carolina, 31" tall. *Courtesy of Don Boring.*

Cloth doll with composition head. *Courtesy of Charlene Upham.*

Another of Mrs. Crinkleton's dolls with sculpted head, feet, and hands. *Courtesy of Jan Lindenberger, Black By Popular Demand, Colorado Springs, Colorado.*

A pair of papier mâché dolls with glass eyes. 12" tall. *Courtesy of Charlene Upham.*

Bisque and Ceramic

Bisque doll with jointed arms and legs, 1860-1870. *Courtesy of Charlene Upham.*

Bisque doll, 7" tall. *Courtesy of Charlene Upham.*

Left: rag doll in chair; right: celluloid doll with open-close glass eyes. *Courtesy of Fran and Jim Pohrer.*

A group of bisque dolls in a wagon. *Courtesy of Fran and Jim Pohrer.*

Painted tin doll head, marked Minerva. *Courtesy of a private collection.*

Two jointed bisque dolls. *Courtesy of a private collection.*

"Baby Phyllis," by Armand Marseille. This 10" doll is rare as a white baby and even rarer as a black baby. She has a stuffed body, porcelain arms and head, and glass eyes. *Courtesy of Kathleen Smith.*

Celluloid and Plastic

Black "Snow White" doll, ca. 1938. *Courtesy of Kathleen Smith.*

This German celluloid doll has the mark of Turtle manufacturers on the back, 6" tall. *Courtesy of Kathleen Smith.*

Plastic and fabric doll with poseable arms and legs. *Courtesy of Jacqueline Peay.*

Jointed celluloid doll. *Courtesy of Jan Lindenberger, Black By Popular Demand, Colorado Springs, Colorado.*

"Amosandra" is a character from the radio show "Amos & Andy" and was copyrighted by CBS. Ruth E. Newton designed her and she was made by the Sun Rubber Co., Barberton, Ohio, 7" tall. *Courtesy of Kathleen Smith.*

Boxing dolls, left to right: Mohammed Ali, Boxing Child, and Apollo Greed. *Courtesy of James Fitzpatrick.*

Left to right: Bell doll, brass and fabric; framed sampler; pipe cleaner and yarn doll. *Courtesy of Conga Colonial.*

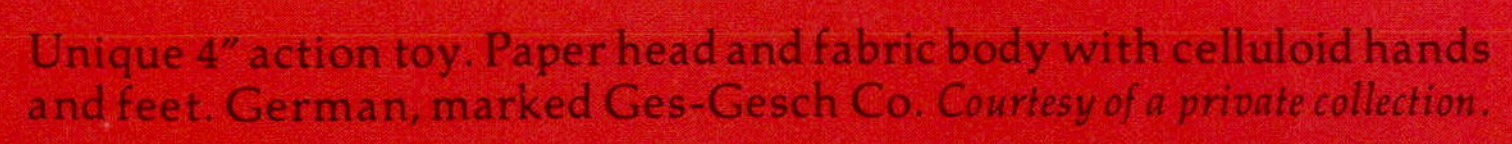

Unique 4" action toy. Paper head and fabric body with celluloid hands and feet. German, marked Ges-Gesch Co. *Courtesy of a private collection.*

Watermelon with doll inside. The watermelon is of painted composition material and the doll is bisque. *Courtesy of Fran and Jim Pohrer.*

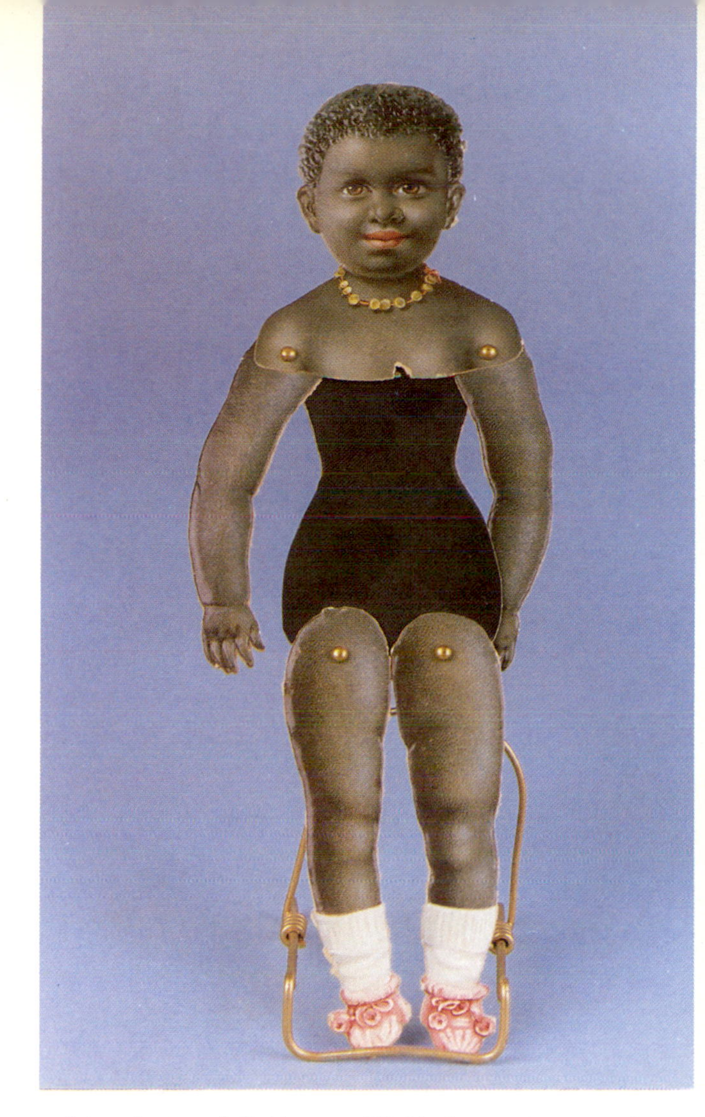

Jointed paper doll. *Courtesy of Holt's Country Store, Grandview, Missouri.*

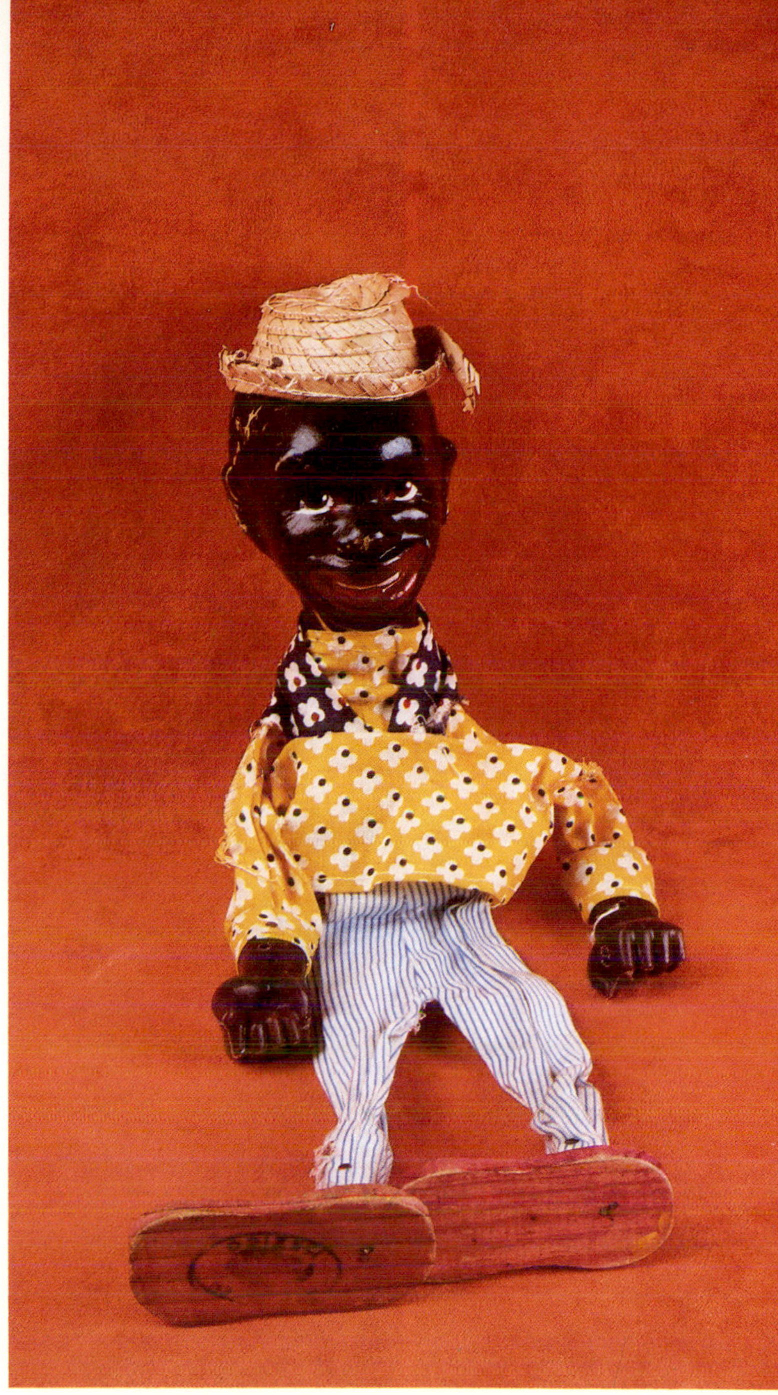

A 15" marionette. *Courtesy of Jan Lindenberger, Black By Popular Demand, Colorado Springs, Colorado.*

"Lester" a ventriloquist's dummy. Plastic and fabric. EEgee Co., 1978. *Courtesy of Don Boring.*

Toys

Black stableman and horse on a rolling platform make up this child's pull-toy. The man and horse are of composition material, and the platform is of wood. 7.5" x 8". *Courtesy of Margaret B. Schiffer.*

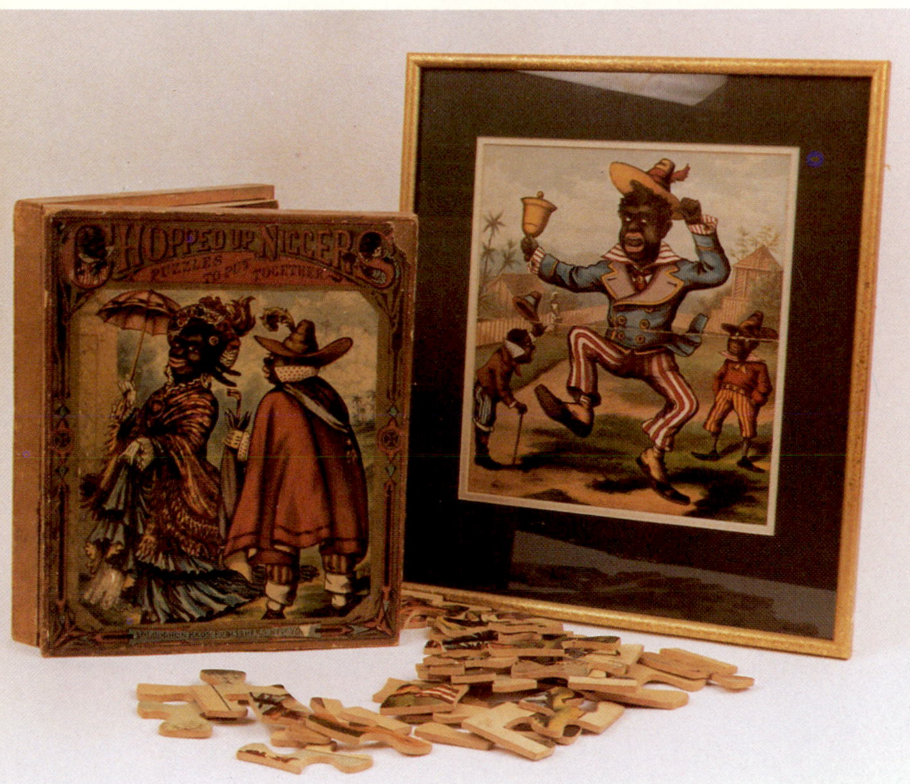

Left: "Chopped Up Niggers—Puzzles to Put Together," McLoughlin Bros. Publishers, New York. Right: Lithograph showing similar stereotyped images. *Courtesy of Fran and Jim Pohrer.*

Puzzle blocks, featuring a bones player, wood and paper. *Courtesy of Holt's Country Store, Grandview, Missouri.*

Paper stretch toy. *Courtesy of Holt's Country Store, Grandview, Missouri.*

Poseable wooden figure of "Andy," copyright Correll & Coborn (?). *Courtesy of Holt's Country Store, Grandview, Missouri.*

Rare candy container with moving mouth. *Courtesy of Holt's Country Store, Grandview, Missouri.*

20" tin shadow dancer painted on both sides. *Courtesy of Elizabeth Holt and Scott Lofquist.*

Two small minstrel Jumping Jacks. Larger: 5.25"; smaller: 4.5". *Courtesy of Margaret B. Schiffer.*

Wooden black Jumping Jack, with its face painted on both sides. 11.75" tall. *Courtesy of Margaret B. Schiffer.*

Black devil puppet of wood and cloth construction. 17.5" tall. *Courtesy of Margaret B. Schiffer.*

"The Nigger Outfit," a grossly exaggerated caricature costume, made in Germany, ca. 1930. *Courtesy of Holt's Country Store, Grandview, Missouri.*

Paper mammy mask. *Courtesy of Holt's Country Store, Grandview, Missouri.*

Left: an accordion player ornament with bisque head and arms and a cloth body, 3.5"; right: pipe-smoking woman ornament with lithographed face and cloth body, 4.25". *Courtesy of Margaret B. Schiffer.*

Paper porter mask. *Courtesy of Holt's Country Store, Grandview, Missouri.*

Left: a carpetbagger ornament; right: an African native. Both are constructed of wire and fabric with composite heads, and are 5.75" inches tall. *Courtesy of Margaret B. Schiffer.*

Games

Target Games

"The Jolly Darkie Target Game," manufactured by Milton Bradley Company, Springfield, Massachusetts, ca. 1890. 15.5" x 12". *Courtesy of Fran and Jim Pohrer.*

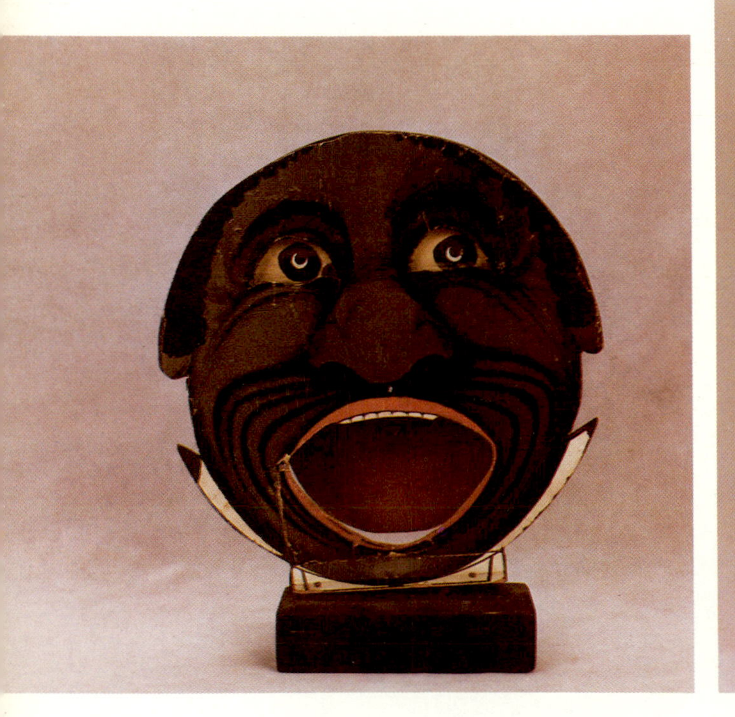

Bean bag toss, ca. 1895. Wood with lithograph, 11" high. American. *Courtesy of Hillman-Gemini Antiques, New York.*

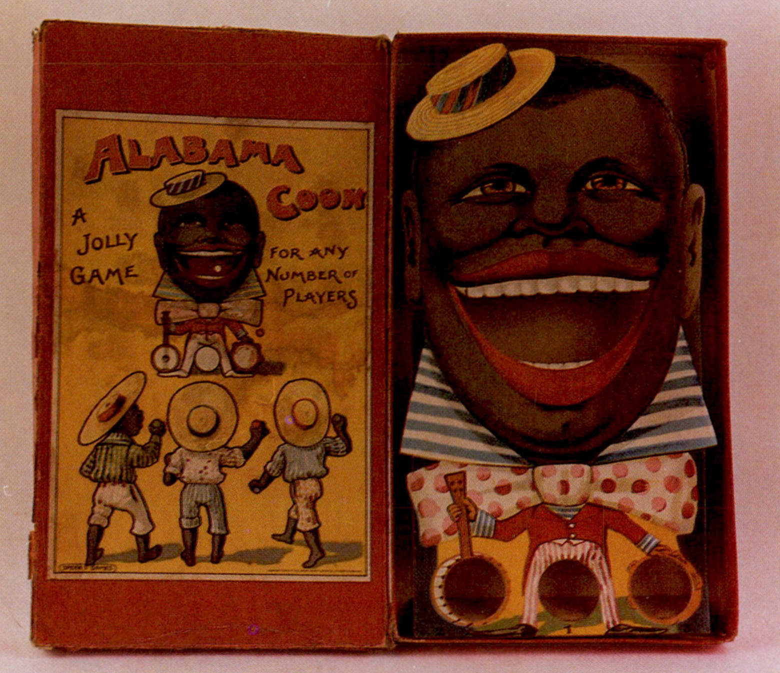

"Alabama Coon-A Jolly Game." This game is nearly identical to the earlier "Jolly Darkie Target Game" by Milton Bradley, right down to the graphics. Manufactured by Spear's Games in Bavaria, "designed" in England. *Courtesy of Holt's Country Store, Grandview, Missouri.*

"Punch & Judy Ten Pins," McLoughlin Bros., New York, copyright 1902. *Courtesy of Holt's Country Store, Grandview, Missouri.*

"Hit the Dodger! Knock Him Out!" A wood and canvas game where the player swings a ball on a string toward the target. 8″ high x 19″ long x 9″ wide. *Courtesy of Boyd Hitchner.*

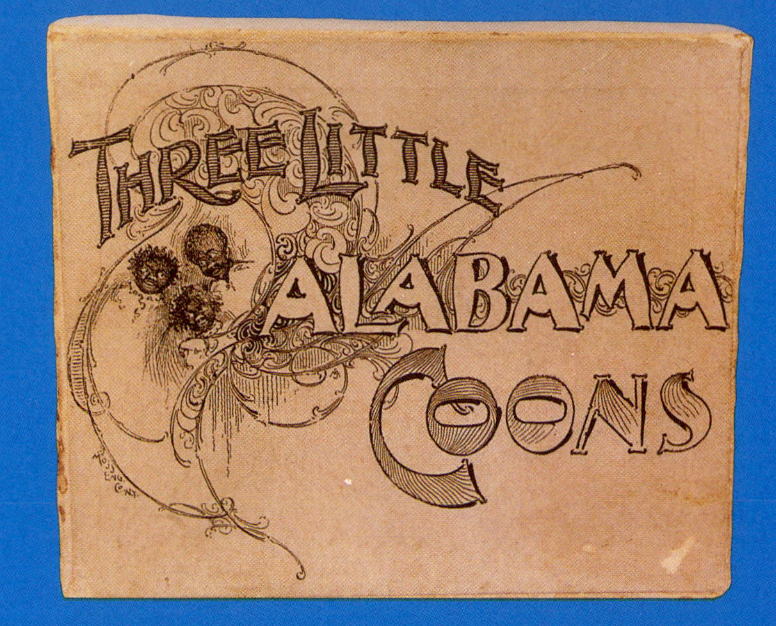

"Three Little Alabama Coons." *Courtesy of Holt's Country Store, Grandview, Missouri.*

Board Games

A black figure is among those trying to climb the ladder of success in this Yellow Kid game. The Yellow Kid was an early and popular newspaper cartoon, generally thought to represent a Chinese immigrant. *Courtesy of a private collection.*

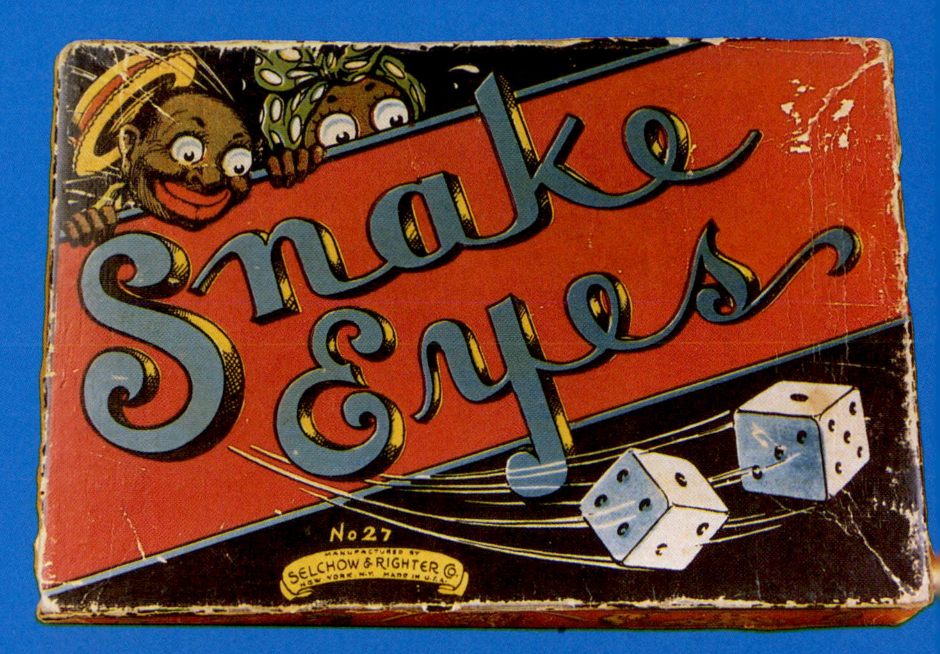

"Snake Eyes," a board game by Selchow & Righter Co., New York. 8″ x 10″, ca. 1930s. *Courtesy of Holt's Country Store, Grandview, Missouri.*

"The Funny Game of Hit or Miss," McLoughlin Bros., New York. While not a target game this has the same theme, being rewarded for hitting the black figure. The spinner is called a "teetotum" and works like a top. *Courtesy of a private collection.*

Books

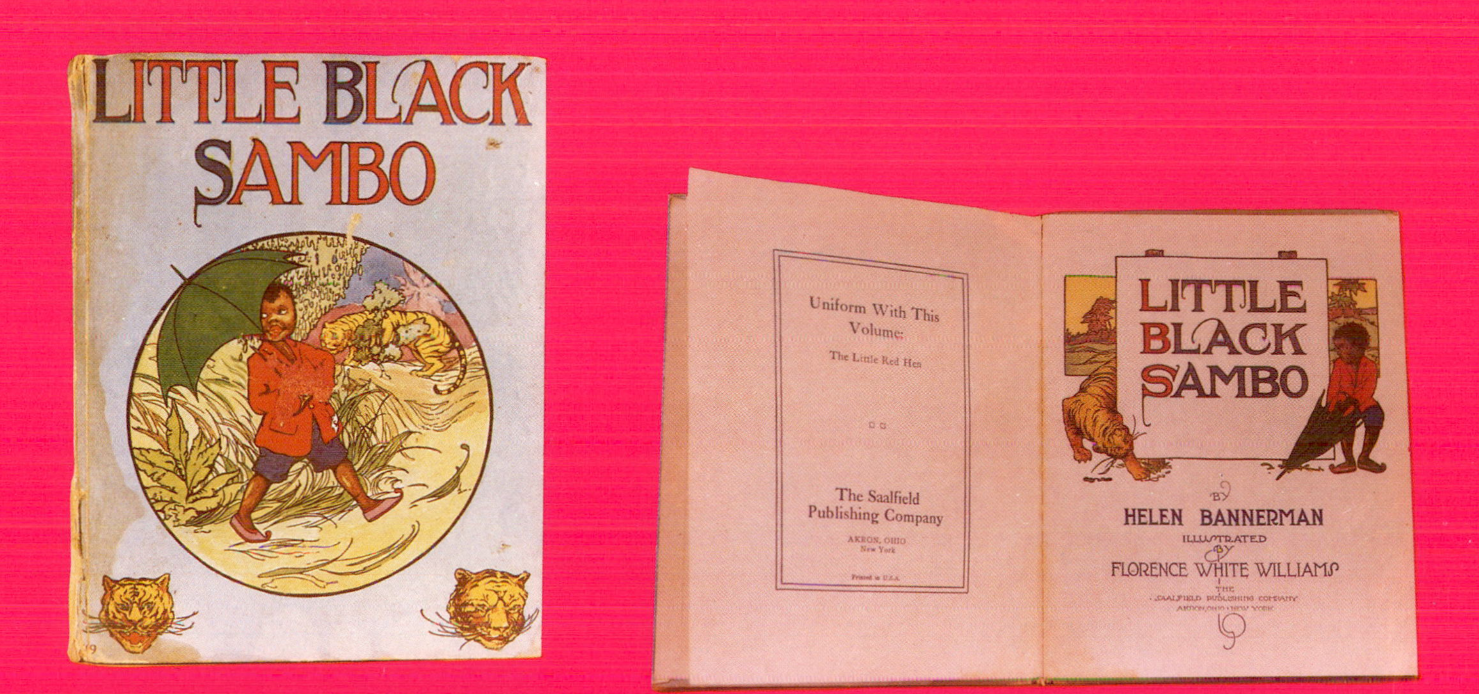

Little Black Sambo, by Helen Bannerman, illustrated by Florence White Williams. Published by the Saalfield Publishing Company, Akron, Ohio. *Courtesy of Holt's Country Store, Grandview, Missouri.*

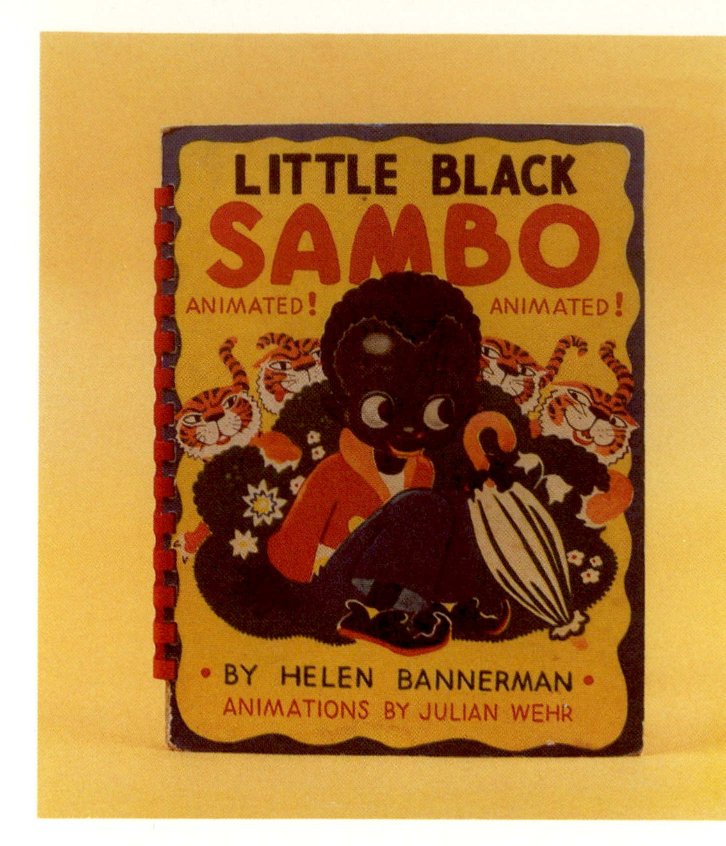

Little Black Sambo, by Helen Bannerman, with animations by Julian Wehr. Plastic bound. *Courtesy of Fran and Jim Pohrer.*

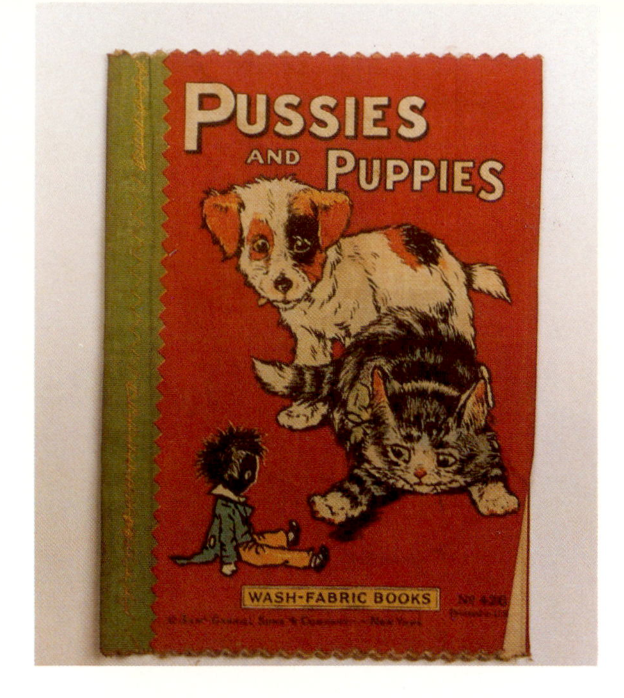

Pussies and Puppies, a washable fabric book published by Samuel Gabriel Sons & Company, New York. It featuresa Golliwogg-type character. *Courtesy of a private collection.*

Naughty Children, by Robert Overton. Published by W. Hagelberg, London and New York. *Courtesy of Holt's Country Store, Grandview, Missouri.*

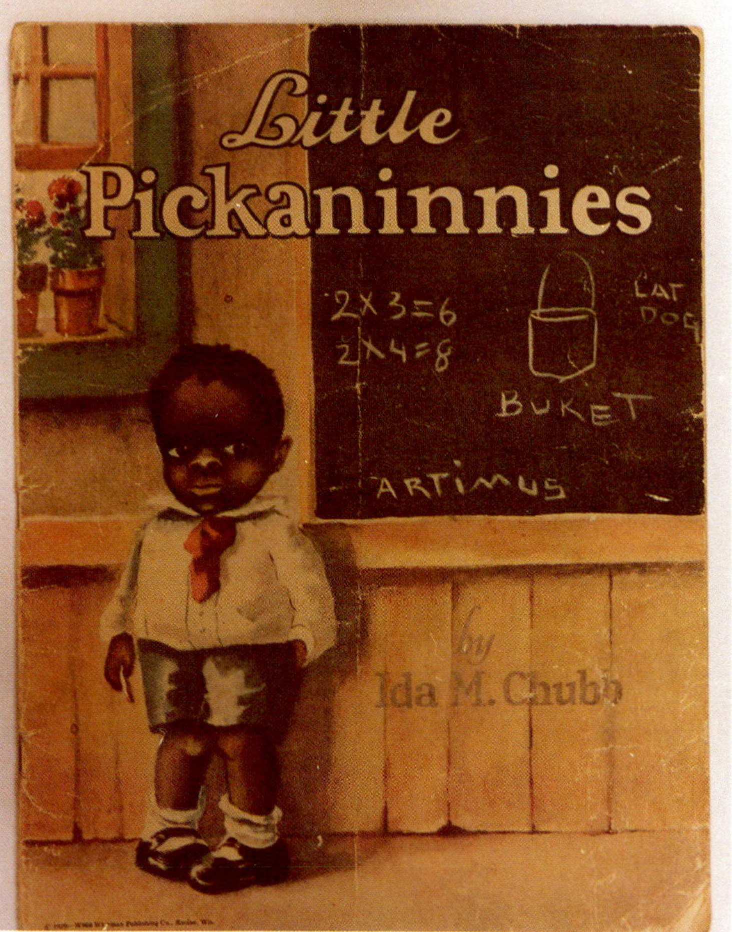

Little Pickaninnies, by Ida M. Chubb. Copyright 1929, Whitman Publishing Co., Racine, Wisconsin. *Courtesy of a private collection.*

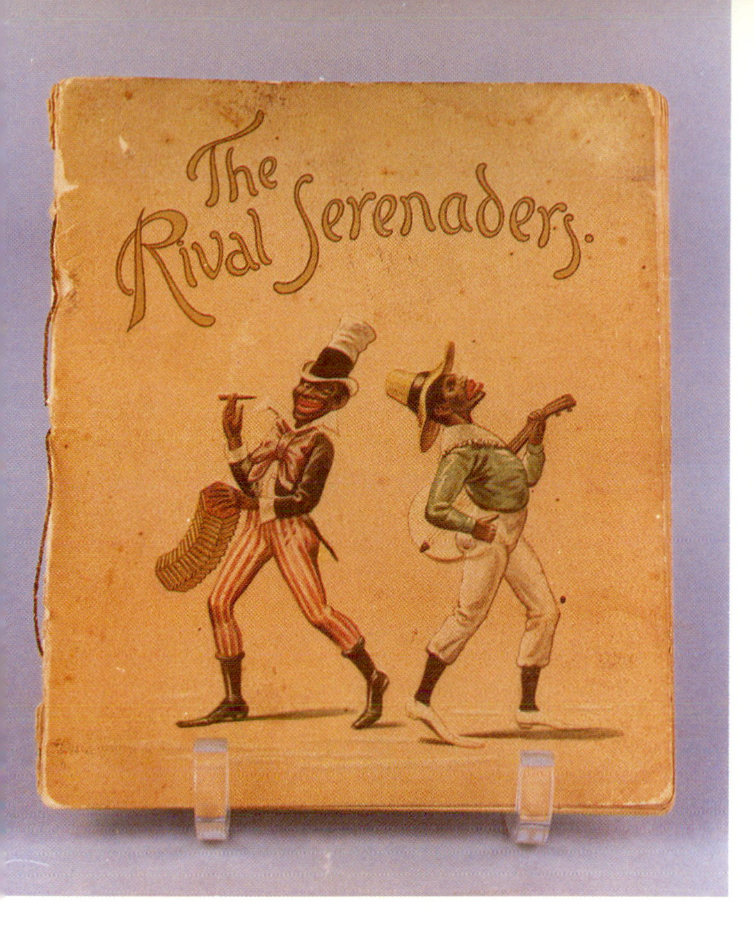

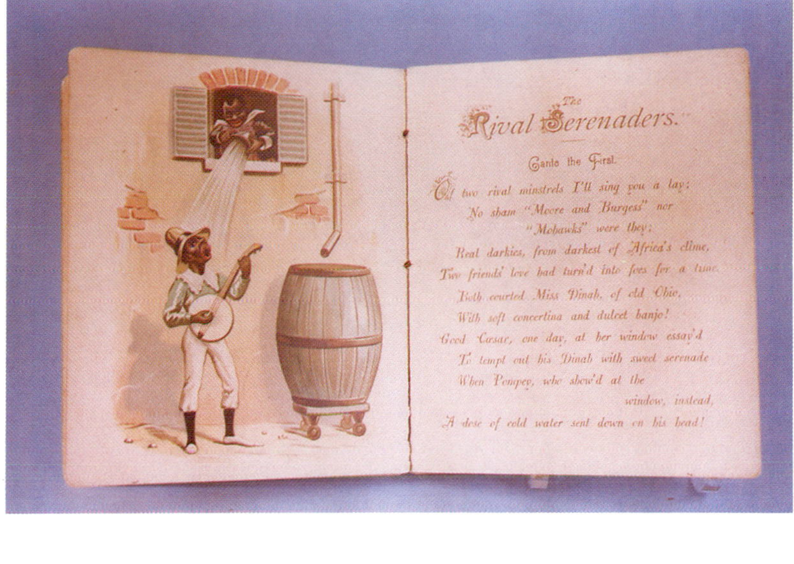
The Rival Serenaders.

Canto the First.

Of two rival minstrels I'll sing you a lay;
No sham "Moore and Burgess" nor
"Mohawks" were they;
Real darkies, from darkest of Africa's clime,
Two friends' love had turn'd into foes for a time.
Both courted Miss Dinah, of old Ohio,
With soft concertina and dulcet banjo!
Good Cæsar, one day, at her window essay'd
To tempt out his Dinah with sweet serenade
When Pompey, who show'd at the
window, instead,
A dose of cold water sent down on his head!

The Rival Serenaders, a long illustrated poem. *Courtesy of Holt's Country Store, Grandview, Missouri.*

Banks

Mechanical bank, cast iron and polychrome, marked "Always Did d'spise a mule." *Courtesy of Jack and Bonita Baldwin.*

"I Always Did 'Spise a Mule," mechanical bank. J. & E. Stevens Co., ca. 1880s. *Schneider's Antique Toys, Lancaster, Pennsylvania.*

Cast iron bank with polychrome finish.

Cast iron bank with traces of paint, 6″ tall. *Courtesy of a private collection.*

Cast iron sharecropper bank with hand painted finish. *Courtesy of Holt's Country Store, Grandview, Missouri.*

Left: Cast iron bank; Right: Cast iron mechanical bank, ca. 1890. *Courtesy of Fran and Jim Pohrer.*

Tin litho wind-up toy. Marked Lindstrom. Made in U.S.A. Says "Mammy" on base. *Courtesy of a private collection.*

"Save and Smile Money Box" cast iron bank manufactured by Sydenham and McCouster, England, 4.5" tall. *Courtesy of John Haley, Halifax, England.*

"Dark Town Battery" cast iron mechanical bank, later reproduced with white players.

"Bad Accident" mechanical bank. *Courtesy of Betty and R.C. Hursman.*

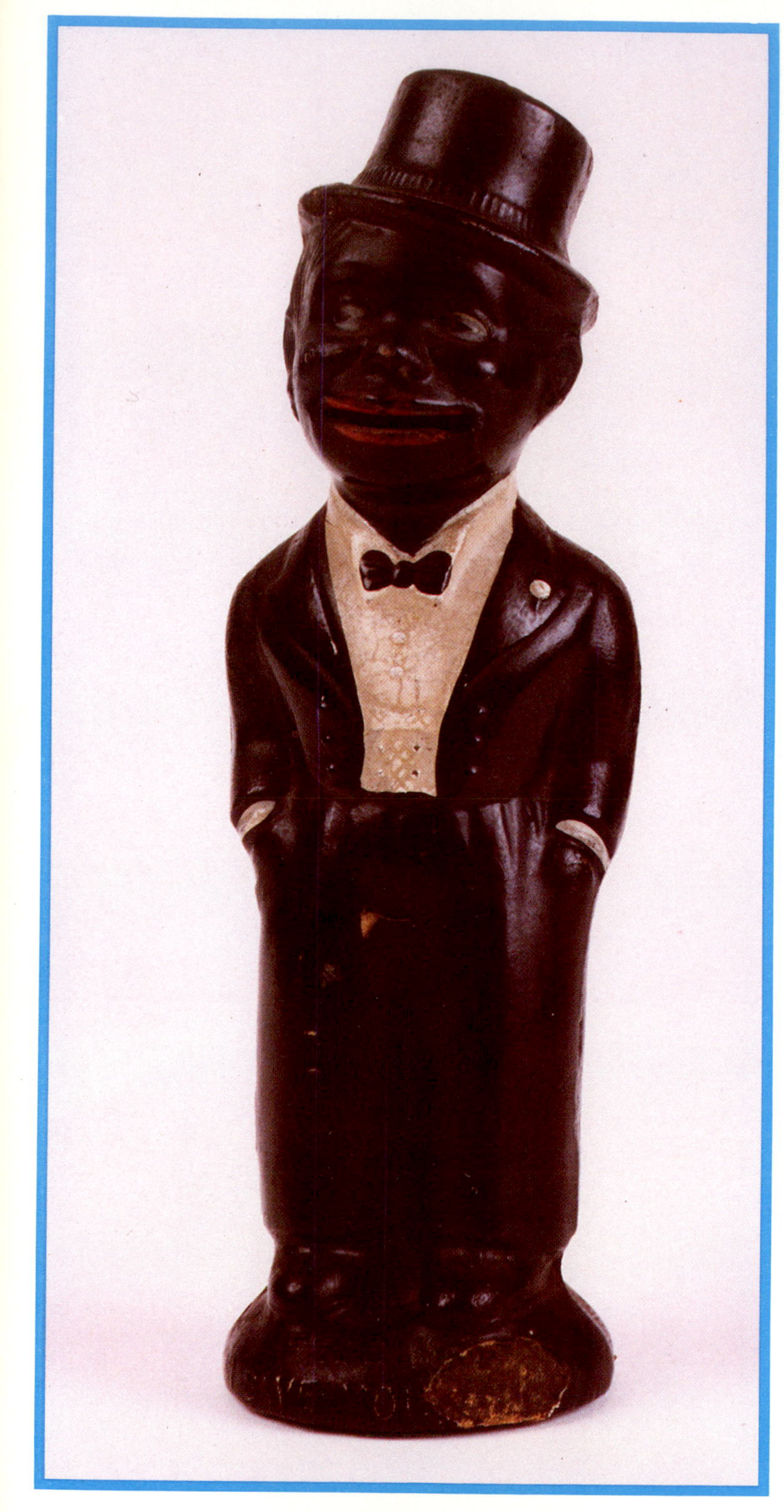

Cast iron bank, marked "Feed me. I save you money." *Courtesy of Renata Ramsbarg Antiques.*

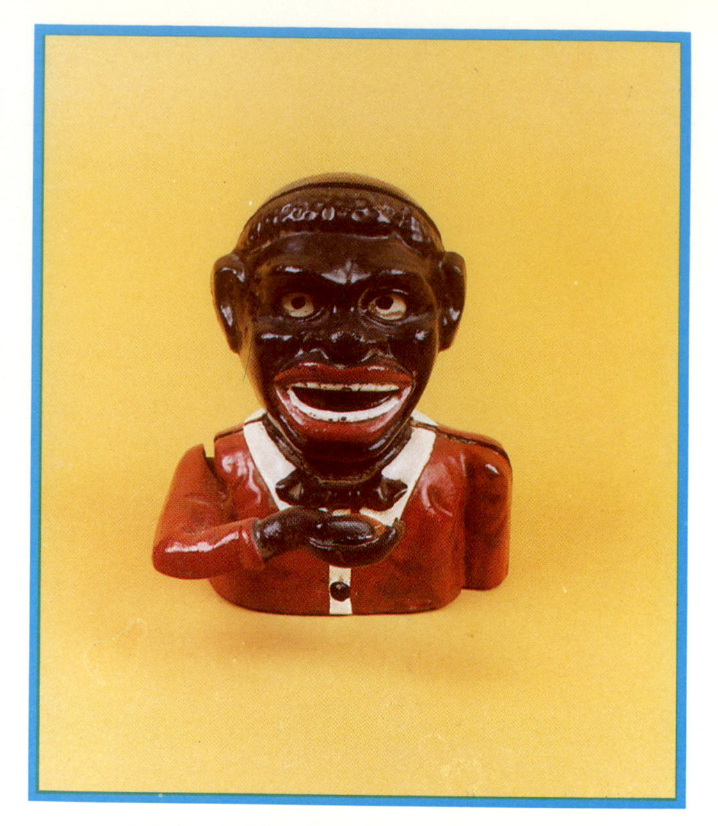

Mechanical bank, cast iron made in three sizes. *Courtesy of Fran and Jim Pohrer.*

Chalkware bank with polychrome finish. *Courtesy of Betty and R.C. Hursman.*

Part Two: Images for Sale

Advertising

Among the earliest appearances of an African-American in commercial advertising was a case of mistaken identity. The cigar store Indian appeared in England around the end of the 1600s, but with a popular confusion that mixed the images of Indian, white settler, and black slave. "As a result," writes Parry, "the wooden figure of a *Black Boy* or *Virginian,* wearing a headdress and kilt of tobacco leaves, instead of feathers, carrying a roll or rope of tobacco under one arm, and holding a long-stem pipe with the opposite hand, became a standard store-front emblem for London tobacco shops" (Parry, 68). The confusion continued until at least the mid-eighteenth century when black "Indians" appeared on the labels of Virginia tobacco shipped to England.

From that time to the present the image of African-Americans has been used to sell many products, often with the same kind of mistaken identity that plagued the earliest advertisers. From tobacco to whiskey, music to stove polish, soap to cereal, black images have touted the goods of an increasingly industrial, consumer-oriented society.

The first large scale use of African-American images in advertising was with the advent of trade cards. Though they had been used before, trade cards experienced their greatest popularity after the introduction of color lithography in about 1870 and before the rise of national magazines. They were used to build brand and store recognition among consumers.

The sizes of the cards varied from small, wallet-size to postcard size and larger. Some, usually for companies, had simple black and white drawings. Others were beautifully colored and represented the best of the lithographer's art. The subjects varied greatly, with sports figures and ethnic humor being two of the most popular themes. The humor was often drawn from other media including newspapers, humor weeklies, minstrelsy, and vaudeville, and was often less than complimentary (*Ethnic Images in Advertising*, p 6).

Black images were used on the trade cards of a variety of products. Often there was no clear connection between the product and the image; the sole purpose of the black person was the humorous situation in which they found themselves. Sometimes there was a certain logic to the use of the image. For example, black figures were commonly used to advertise soap and stove polish. In soap advertisements one would often see the product being used to wash away the black skin color, while stove polish had the opposite use, making white skin black.

The popularity of trade cards was greatest between 1870 and 1900. After the turn of the century they were displaced by the rise of national magazines and the wide-reaching advertising they offered. During their heyday trade cards were avidly collected by both children and adults, which may account for their availability to collectors today.

By 1905 there were twenty general monthly magazines with national of over 100,000. Priced at ten to fifteen cents per issue, they were affordable

1910 advertisement for Cream of Wheat. The artist is not named, but this is likely an early work by Edward V. Brewer who would continue a long relationship with Cream of Wheat. *Courtesy of Holt's Country Store, Grandview, Missouri.*

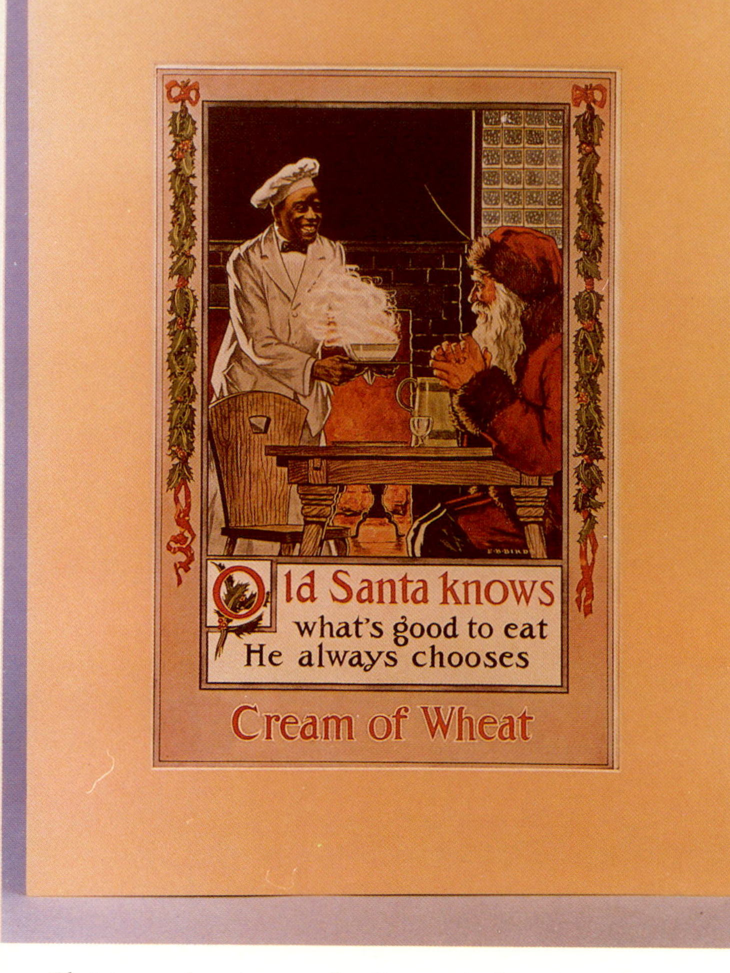

Christmas advertisement for Cream of Wheat drawn by E.B. Bird. *Courtesy of Holt's Country Store, Grandview, Missouri.*

Full color advertisement on paper. Painted by Benton ca. 1907. *Courtesy of Holt's Country Store, Grandview, Missouri.*

and quite popular, and a perfect vehicle for advertisers who sought an easy, effective way to reach the largest number of people (*Ethnic Images in Advertising*, p.7).

The image of black people in magazine advertising was quite different from that in trade cards. The most offensive images disappeared along with much of the ethnic humor that used black people as the butt of the joke. One of the factors in this change was the growing recognition of the buying power in the black community and the desire not to offend. Another had to do with the national character of the magazines and need to find images that appealed to a variety of sensibilities.

In the advertising of magazines and other media at the turn of the century, the most commonly used image of African-Americans was that of servant. Porters, chefs, maids, and butlers were used to promote a variety of products. In large part these were variations on the "Uncle" and "Mammy" characters that found such popularity with the audiences of minstrel shows in the nineteenth century.

Cream of Wheat and Aunt Jemima used black people as the central representatives of their products. The Cream of Wheat advertisements featured "Rastus" as a smiling, friendly chef who, either in person or staring from a ad-within-an-ad, was always ready with a steaming bowl of Cream of Wheat. The "Rastus" figure was a breakthrough of sorts. Like the Gold Dust Twins of Fairbanks Soaps, black images had been used by other companies as trademarks for their products. Almost without exception, however, the figures were highly exaggerated physically and placed in stereotypical roles and situations. While not escaping the servant role, sympathetic character of Rastus is drawn realistically...except for his ever-present smile. This represents a small, but significant gain.

The figure of Aunt Jemima gives insight into how the black images used in advertising have changed during this century. When the pancake mix was introduced at the Columbian Exhibition in Chicago in 1893, Nancy Green, a black cook from Kentucky played the part of Aunt Jemima. She continued the role until her death in 1923. Despite this "real" Aunt Jemima, the image used in

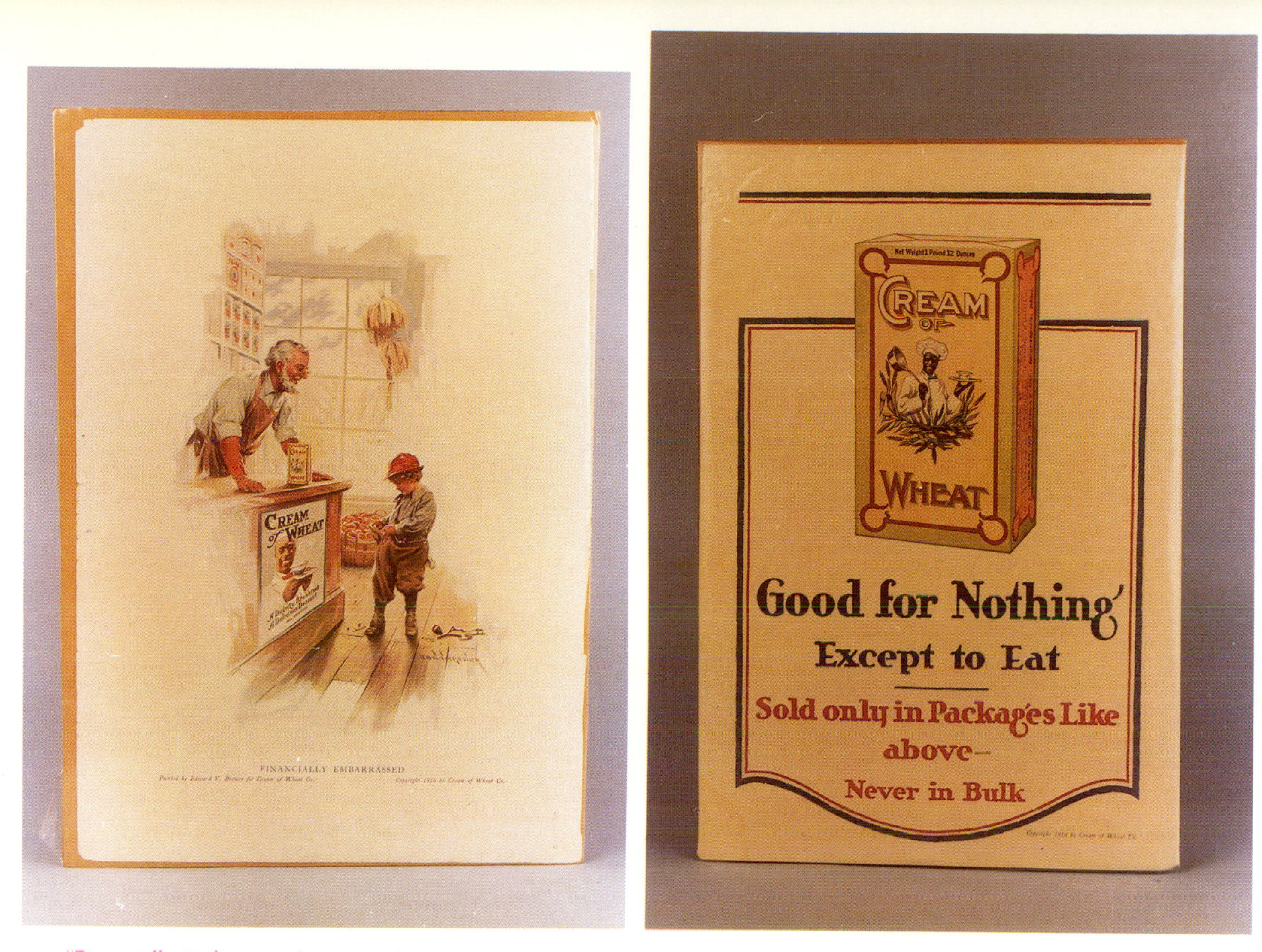

"Financially Embarrassed." Poster by Edward V. Brewer, 1916. *Courtesy of Holt's Country Store, Grandview, Missouri.*

"Good for Nothing Except to Eat." Poster, 1916. *Courtesy of Holt's Country Store, Grandview, Missouri.*

advertising and packaging from the beginning until 1917 was more stereotypical than realistic. A new, more accurate image of Aunt Jemima was adopted by the company in 1917. The physical representation of Aunt Jemima has continued to evolve as the tastes of the culture have changed. Today her image is limited to a small oval on the package showing a slimmer, younger woman, more like a housewife than a servant (though some would argue at the distinction).

The packaging of products also underwent significant changes at the end of the nineteenth century. In the early years of the century most items were sold in bulk, and any concern with "point of purchase advertising" was limited to labels or the decorations on large crates or boxes. As brand names became more popular and items began to be stocked in individual packages, the importance of packaging grew. Well-designed, colorful wrappings and boxes became an integral part of a products marketing.

As with print advertising, black images were used on a variety of packaging. Food products, tobacco, and coffee were the most popular. P.J. Gibbs points out, however, that any product that was black or white, or had black or white in its name, was likely to make use of the black image in its advertising (Gibbs, *Black Collectibles Sold in America*, p. 120).

The covers to sheet music were another packaging effort that used black images. They are evidence both to the contribution of black people to popular music and the strength of the stereotype of the innate musicality of the African-American.

Advertising has the functions of reflection and projection. To be effective it must measure the attitudes, values, and beliefs of its audience and reflect them back in support of the product it is promoting. At the same time it must project new values, new attitudes, new desires if it is attain its goal of expanding the marketplace. In that sense advertising has had a role in changing a society's sense of itself and of those who are a part of it. From the history of advertising in the last 150 years we can see both the reflective and projective functions and how they have impacted the American attitudes toward race.

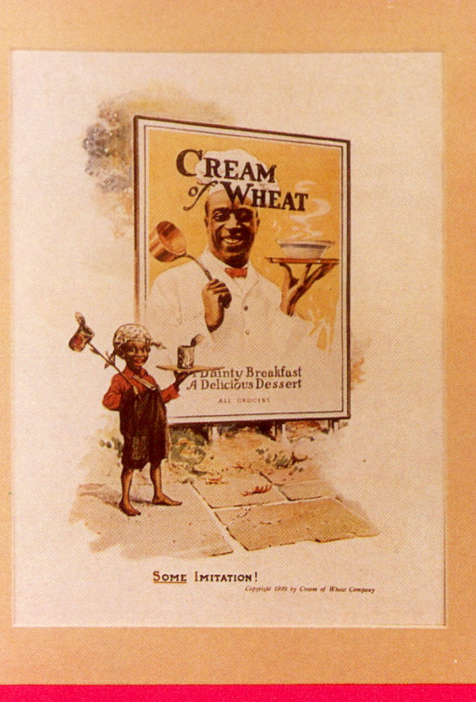

"Some Imitation!" Poster, artist unknown, 1920. *Courtesy of Holt's Country Store, Grandview, Missouri.*

"Giddap, Uncle." A socially revealing poster by Edward V. Brewer, 1921. *Courtesy of Holt's Country Store, Grandview, Missouri.*

"My Cream of Wheat, You Rascal." Edward V. Brewer. *Courtesy of Holt's Country Store, Grandview, Missouri.*

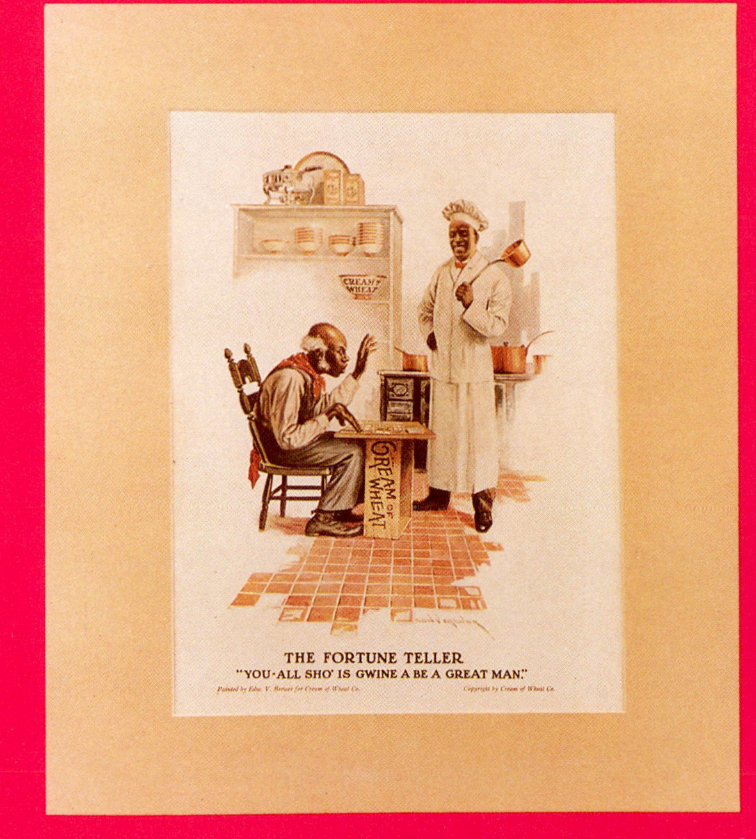

"The Fortune Teller." Edward V. Brewer, ca. 1921. *Courtesy of Holt's Country Store, Grandview, Missouri.*

"His Bodyguard." Two color poster by Edward V. Brewer. *Courtesy of Holt's Country Store, Grandview, Missouri.*

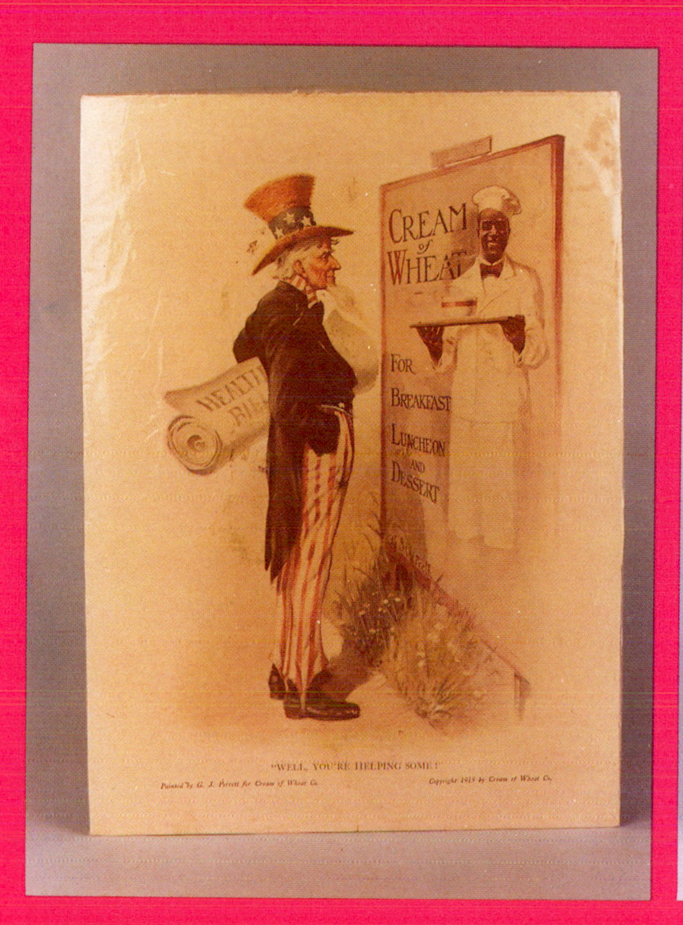

"Well, You're Helping Some!" Poster by G.J. Perrett, 1915. *Courtesy of Holt's Country Store, Grandview, Missouri.*

"To the Queen's Taste." Edward V. Brewer, 1923. *Courtesy of Holt's Country Store, Grandview, Missouri.*

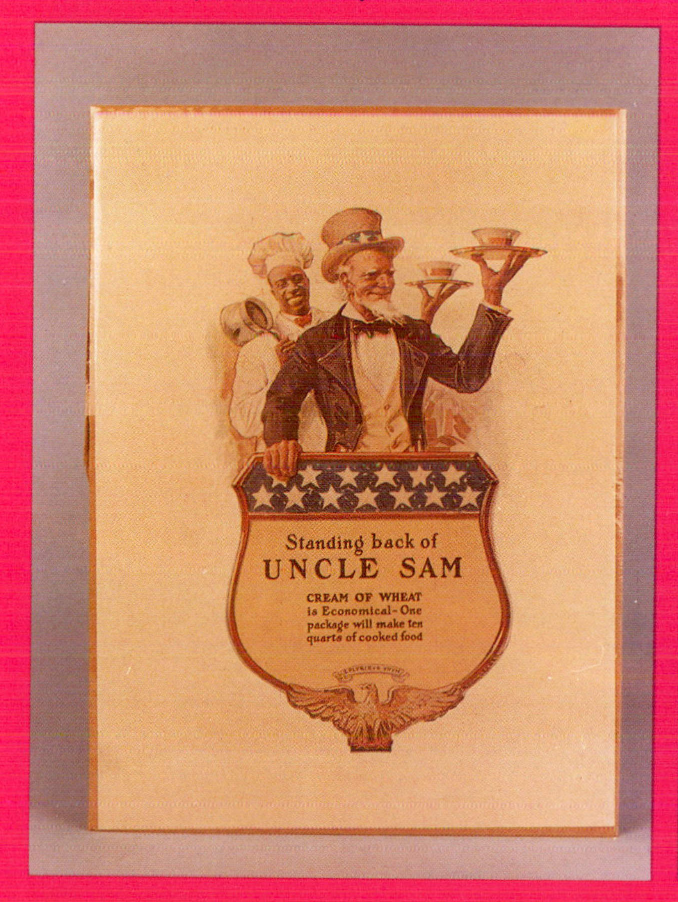

"Standing Back of Uncle Sam." Artist unknown. *Courtesy of Holt's Country Store, Grandview, Missouri.*

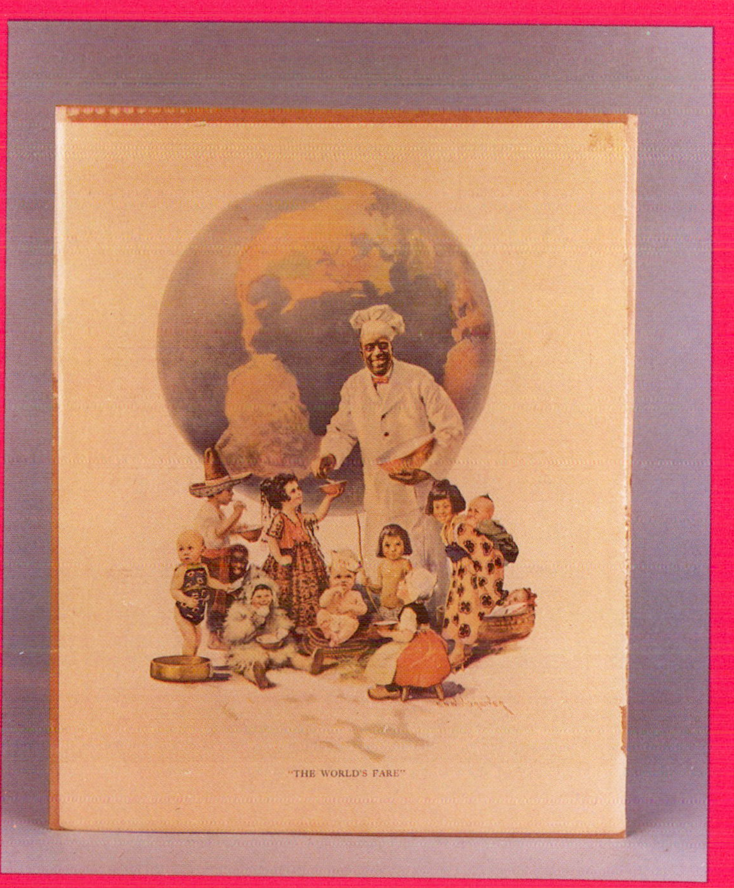

"The World's Fare." Edward V. Brewer. *Courtesy of Holt's Country Store, Grandview, Missouri.*

Weather Bird Shoes paper advertisement. Pulling the tab causes the eyes and mouth to open. *Courtesy of Holt's Country Store, Grandview, Missouri.*

Lithographed tin advertisement for Clover Brand Shoes. *Courtesy of Holt's Country Store, Grandview, Missouri.*

Paper advertisement for Diamond Brand shoes by the Peters Shoe Co, St. Louis. Marked with a "D" in a diamond and the numbers 1047 in the lower left corner. *Courtesy of Holt's Country Store, Grandview, Missouri.*

"The Aunt Jemima Needle Book" contained needles and offers for a rag doll family. The Aunt Jemima Mills Company (Davis Mills), ca. 1905. 2.75" high. *Courtesy of Holt's Country Store, Grandview, Missouri.*

Aunt Jemima banner pin. "I'se in town honey" was given a trademark in 1916, though it was in use as early as 1905. Davis sold Aunt Jemima to Quaker Oats in 1925. The pin is linen attached to a metal bar. 1922. *Courtesy of Holt's Country Store, Grandview, Missouri.*

A lithographed metal pin, ca. 1949. *Courtesy of Holt's Country Store, Grandview, Missouri.*

It looks as though Aunt Jemima has shifted her loyalties, but in fact Kellogg is playing on the image of quality the mammy figure had come to represent. This advertisement ran in the September, 1930 issue of *Good Housekeeping* magazine. H. K. Kellogg, Battle Creek, Michigan.

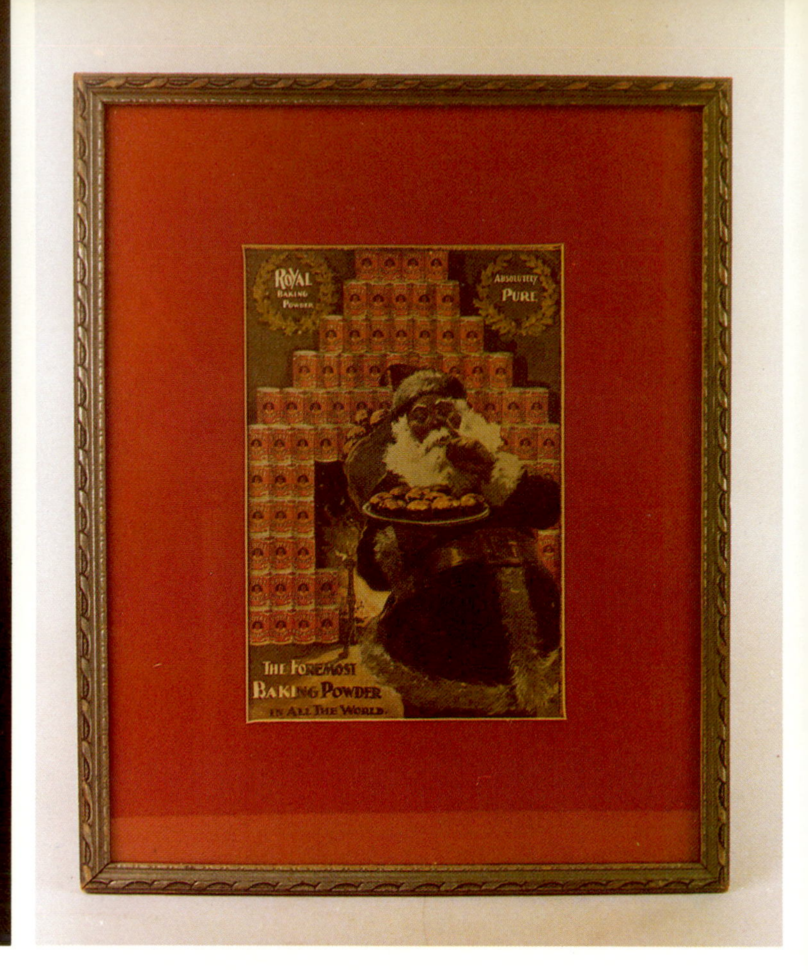

It is unclear whether this is black Santa or a soot-covered white Santa, though the latter is more likely. An advertisement for Royal Baking Powder, ca. 1910. *Courtesy of Holt's Country Store, Grandview, Missouri.*

At first glance this advertising calendar from Nestlés food seems remarkable for its integration. A closer look, however, shows that it is truly remarkable for its lack of subtlety. Entitled "Coming Events Cast Their Shadows Before," the calendar foretells the futures of these children by the symbols above their heads. The white children are clearly destined to greatness: lawyer, bishop, gentleman, soldier, lady, millionaire, scholar, etc. The black child, however, has only a question mark to cast its doubtful destiny. Lithographed paper, ca. 1894. *Courtesy of Holt's Country Store, Grandview, Missouri.*

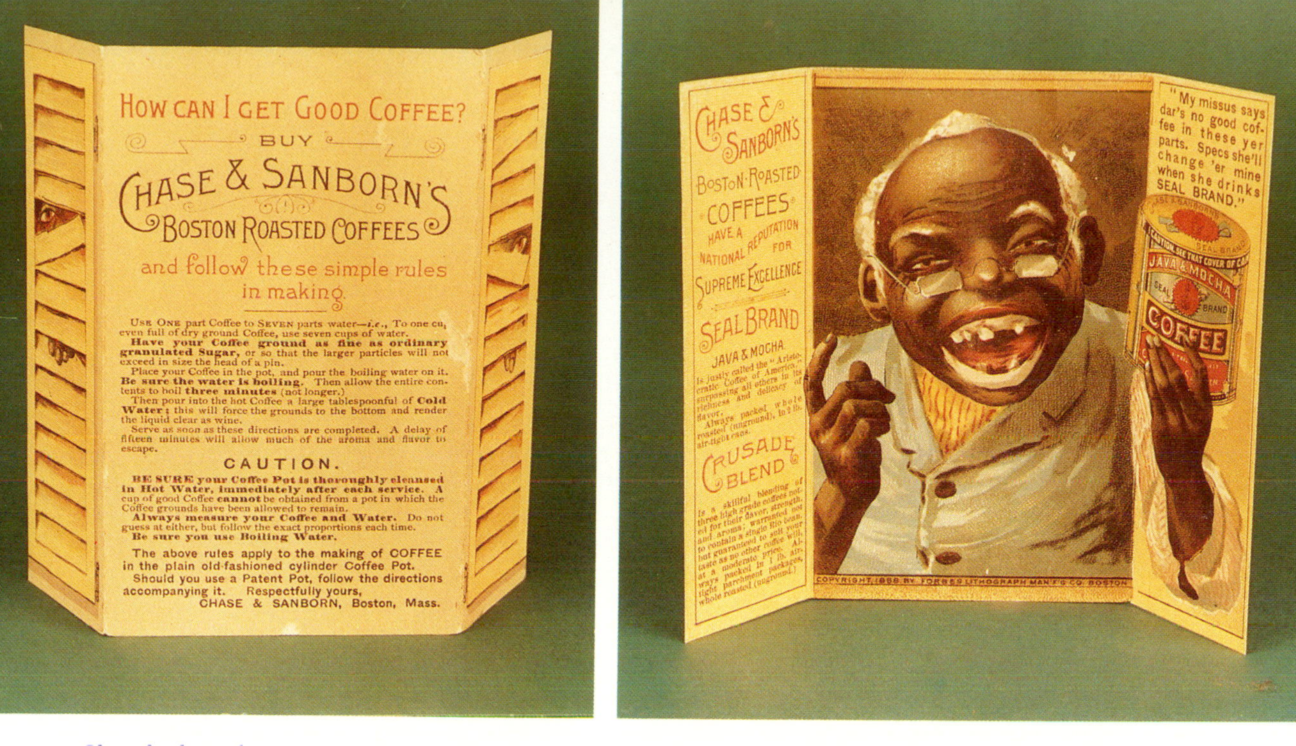

Closed, this Chase & Sanborn advertising card shows eyes peering through the slates of the window shutters. When opened, the nearly toothless person hawks Chase & Sanborn's Seal Brand Boston roasted coffee. Copyright 1888 by Forbes Lithograph Manufacturing Co., Boston. *Courtesy of a private collection.*

A lithographed tin sign for Picaninny Freeze, "A Pal for Your Palate." Hendlers Ice Cream, ca. 1922. *Courtesy of Holt's Country Store, Grandview, Missouri.*

Oval lithographed tin Pepsi advertising sign, ca. 1960s. *Courtesy of Jack and Lettie Pennington, Mocksville, North Carolina.*

Alcohol

Cardboard advertising sign for Paul Jones & Co., Louisville, Kentucky.

A large (24″) tin tray advertising Green River Whiskey, "Whiskey Without A Headache." Chas. Shonk Co., Chicago, ca. 1885. *Courtesy of Ken Aubrey.*

Lithographed tin sign for Fern Glen Rye. Fern Glen Distilling Company, East St. Louis, Illinois, ca. 1890. *Courtesy of Holt's Country Store, Grandview, Missouri.*

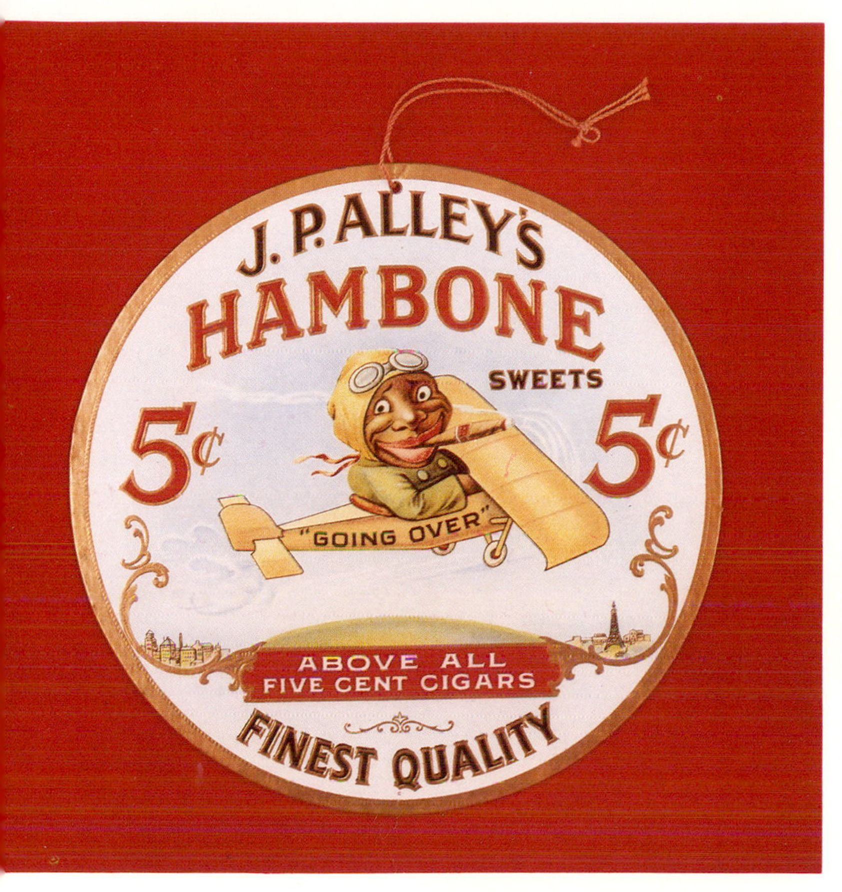

Tin sign for J. Palley's Hambone Sweets, ca. 1910. *Courtesy of Don Flanagan.*

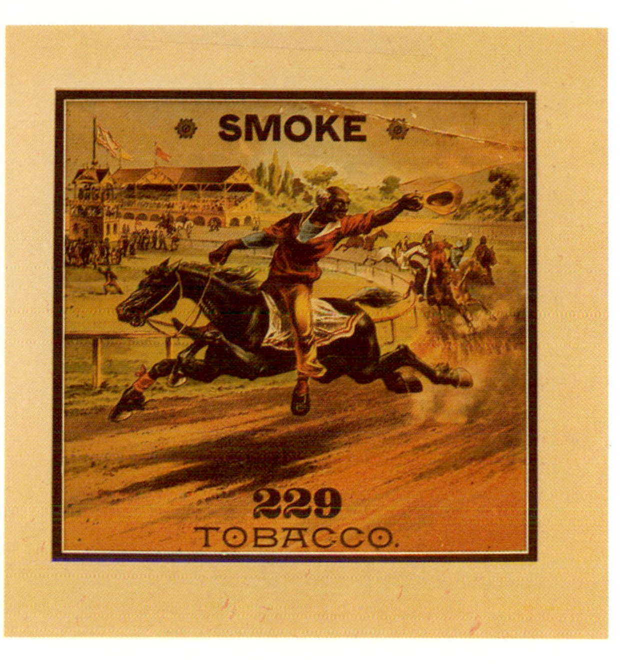

Advertisement for 229 Tobacco, 12" x 12". *Courtesy of House of Stuart, Centerport, New York.*

Sign for Lime Kiln Club Tobacco. J. Bagley & Co., Detroit, ca. 1890. Printed by the Detroit Lithographic Co. 12" x 15". *Courtesy of House of Stuart, Centerport, New York.*

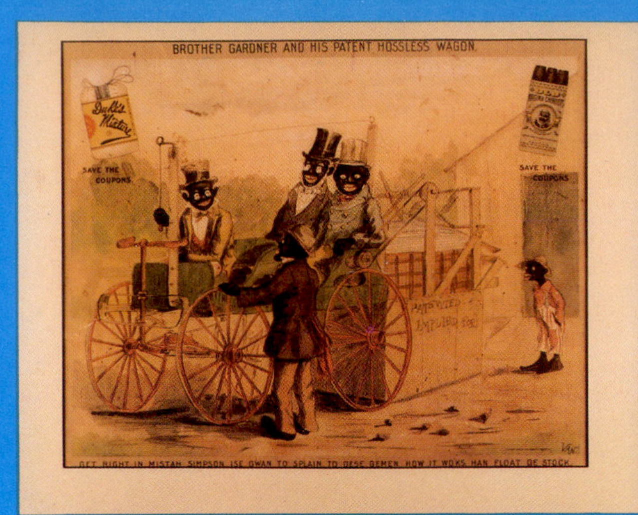

1. "Get right in Mistah Simpson. Ise gwan to splain to dese gemen how it woks han float de stock." *Courtesy of Neat Olde Things, Stewartsville, New Jersey.*

2. "Sit still gemen. Its only de lectricity cracking. It stats up kindah sudden.

3. "Scuse me Mistah Gardner, but lectricity doan gree wi me no how."

4. (Bro. Gardner): "Da seems to be a pow'ful sight ob lectricity in de biler." (*Soto voce*): "I'll bet dat yanimals jus humpin his sef now."

5. "Je-e-rusalem-de-golden! Dat must be one o' dem flyin machines comin."

6. "For de Lawd! Dis mus be what dat nigger ment when he said he'd float de stock."

"Brother Gardner and His Patent Hossless Wagon," six-episode comic advertisement for Old Virginia Cheroots and Duke's Mixture. ©, signed VAN.

Trade Cards

Trade cards for Fairbanks soaps showing a variety of styles. The pose of the twins at the bottom was to become the Gold Dust logo. *Courtesy of Holt's Country Store, Grandview, Missouri.*

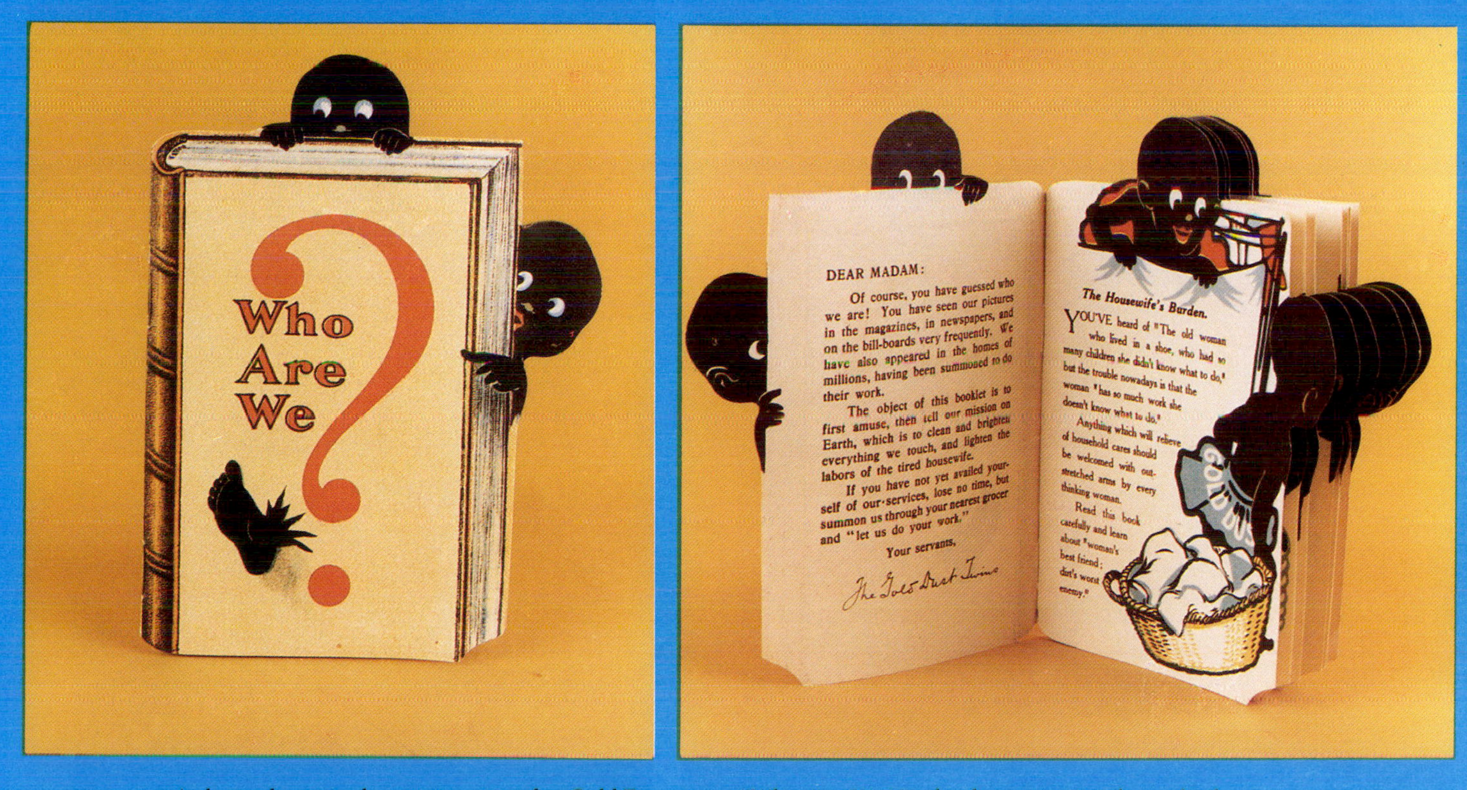

A clever die-cut advertising piece for Gold Dust soap. "Who Are We?" asks the cover. Inside we find what we've already guessed, the Gold Dust Twins. The purpose of the book, they tell us, is "to first amuse, then tell our mission on Earth, which is to clean and brighten everything we touch, and lighten the burdens of the tired housewife." It is signed, "Your servants, The Gold Dust Twins." *Courtesy of Fran and Jim Pohrer.*

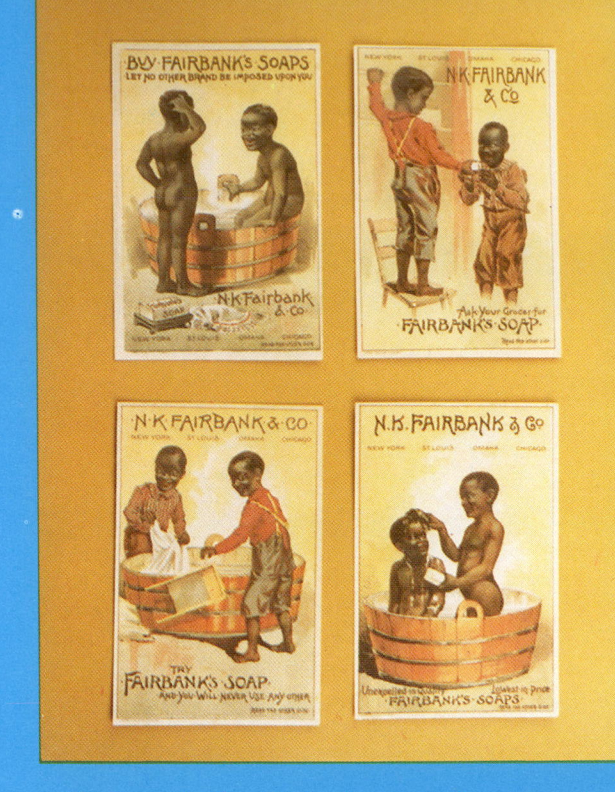

Trade cards for Fairbanks soaps featuring the Fairbanks Twins. The twins later became the Gold Dust Twins and acted as the logo for Fairbanks Gold Dust Washing Powder. N.K. Fairbanks & Co., New York, St. Louis, Omaha, and Chicago. *Courtesy of Holt's Country Store, Grandview, Missouri.*

Assorted trade cards (clockwise from top left): "Aunty Fat and Auntie Lean;" Red Cross Granulated Lye, Thomson & Taylor Spice Co., Chicago; Reid's Celebrated Flower Seeds; Ayer's Cathartic Pills, copyright 1881. *Courtesy of Holt's Country Store, Grandview, Missouri.*

Trade cards (clockwise from top left): Gold Dust Washing Powder, N.K. Fairbank & Co.; an unknown corn product; Northrup, King & Co.'s seeds, C.J.A. Landbourg, Minneapolis, Minnesota and Berkeley, California; Harden's Seeds, Kansas City, Missouri, copyright 1888 by Charles Brown. *Courtesy of Holt's Country Store, Grandview, Missouri.*

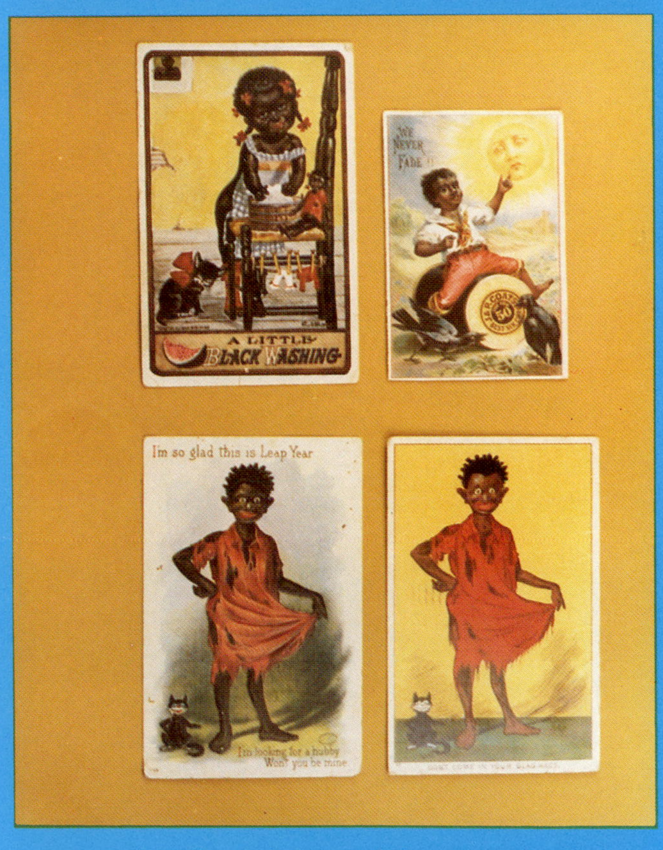

Assorted trade cards : top left, "A Little Black Washing," product unknown; top right, "We Never Fade," J.P. Coats thread; bottom, two greeting cards using the same image but different captions. *Courtesy of Holt's Country Store, Grandview, Missouri.*

Assorted trade cards: Minstrel, marked Raphael Tuck & Sons; "A Few of the World's Fair," Hood's Sasparilla, copyright 1891 by C.I. Hood & Co.; "The Christening," signed Francis Brundage. *Courtesy of a private collection.*

Other Advertisements

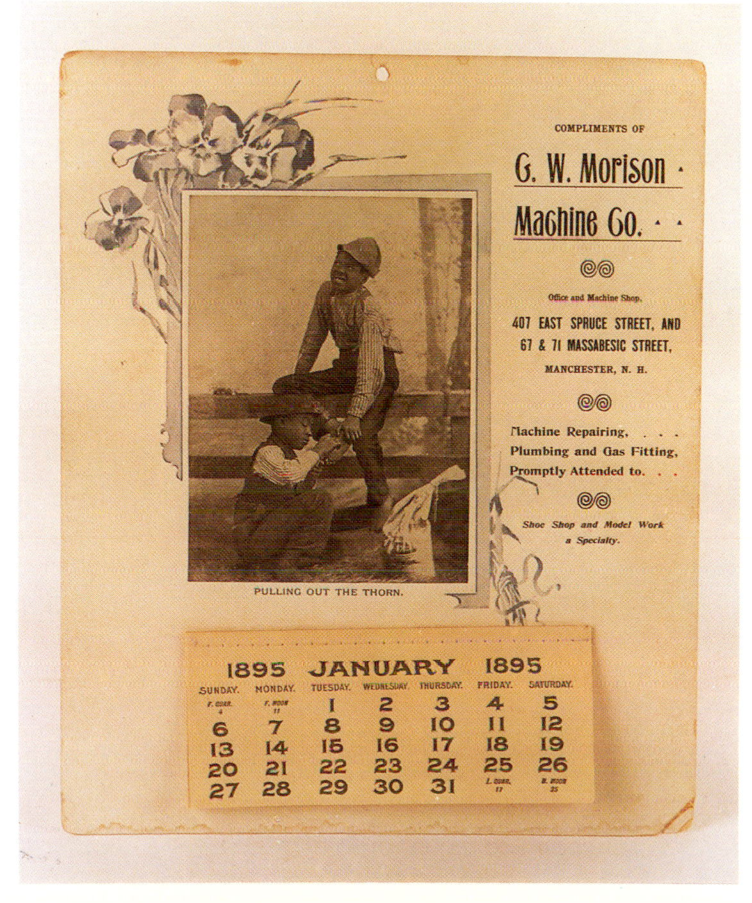

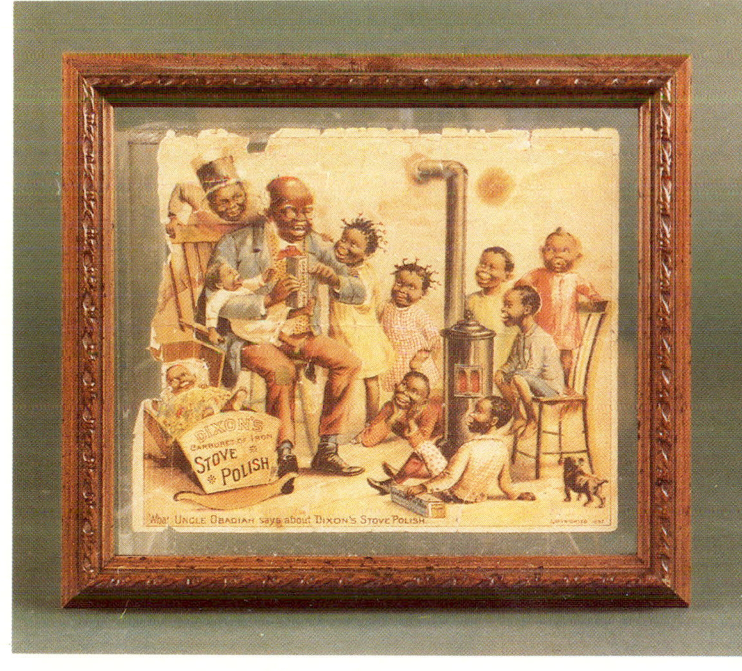

Advertisement for Dixon's Carburet of Iron Stove Polish, featuring Uncle Obadiah, copyright 1892. *Courtesy of Elizabeth Holt and Scott Lofquist.*

Calendar from the G.W. Morrison Machine Company, Manchester, New Hampshire, 1895. *Courtesy of Holt's Country Store, Grandview, Missouri.*

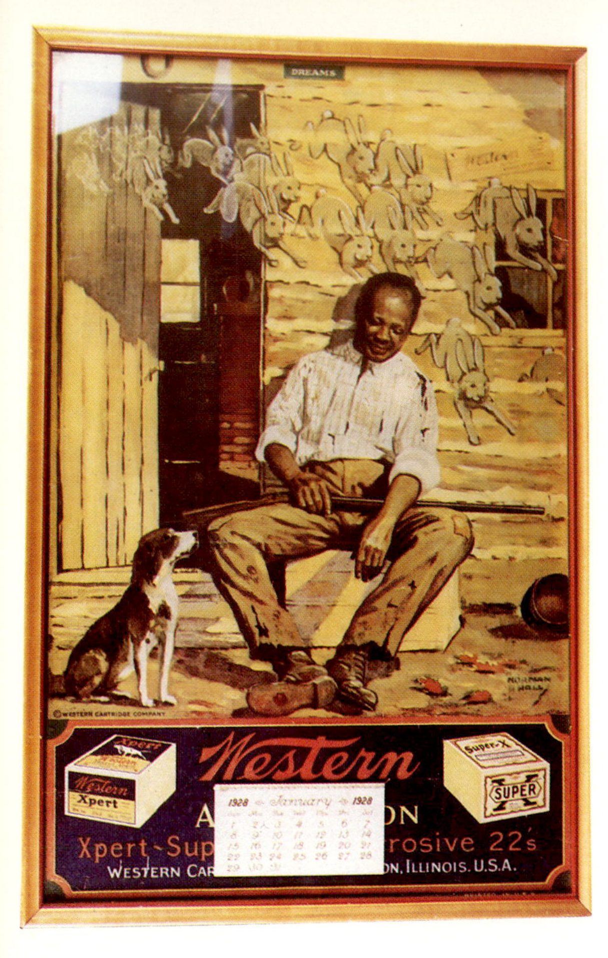

Calendar advertising Western Ammunition, Western Cartridge Company, 1928. The art work by Norman Hall is entitled "Dreams." *Courtesy of Steven Still.*

Comic advertisement from Bernheim Distributing Co., Louisville, KY. "Honey Does Yo Lub Yo Man?" was copyrighted by Knaffl & Bro., Knoxville, Tennessee, 1897. *Courtesy of Holt's Country Store, Grandview, Missouri.*

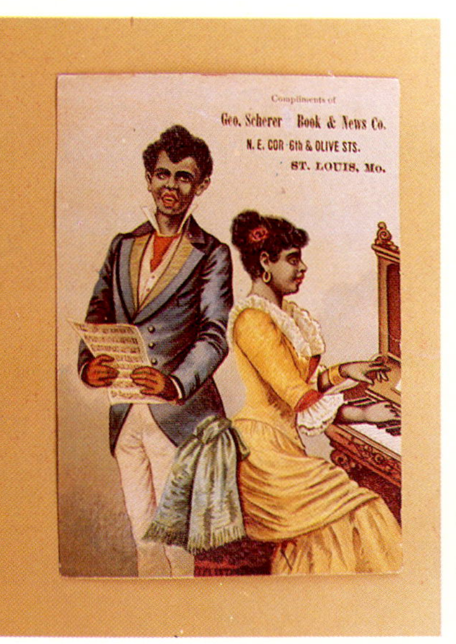

Advertisement for Geo. Scherer Book and News Company, St. Louis, Missouri. *Courtesy of Holt's Country Store, Grandview, Missouri.*

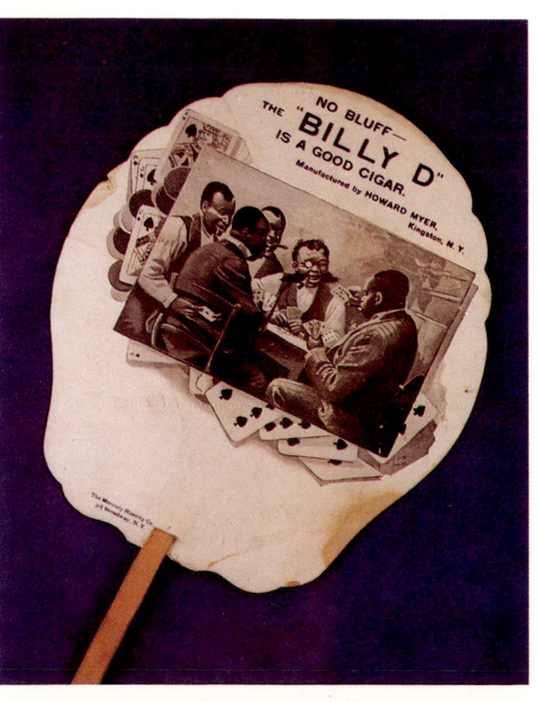

Advertising fan for the "Billy D" cigar, manufactured by Howard Myer, Kingston, New York. The fan was made by Mercury Novelty Co., New York, ca. 1930. *Courtesy of Neat Olde Things, Stewartsville, New Jersey.*

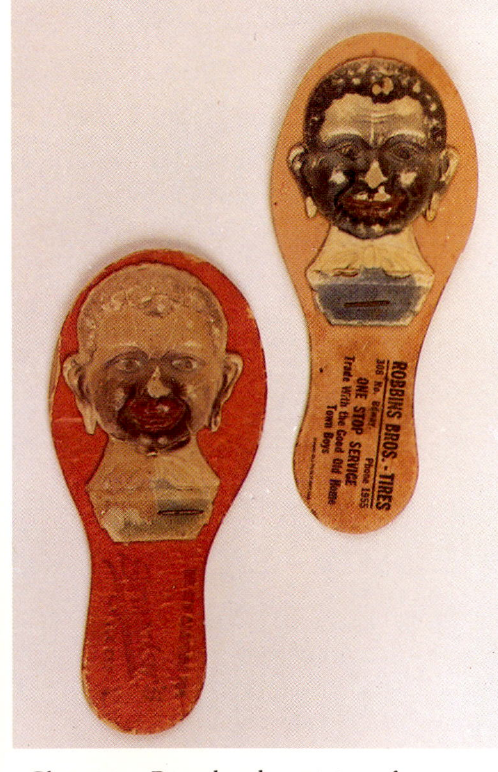

Clapping Board advertising for Robbins Bros.—Tires (top), and Snyder's Ice Cream. By shaking the board back and forth, the face would make a clapping sound as it hit against the board. *Courtesy of Elizabeth Holt and Scott Lofquist*

Luzianne Coffee tin pail. *Courtesy of Holt's Country Store, Grandview, Missouri.*

Luzianne Coffee tin pail. *Courtesy of Holt's Country Store, Grandview, Missouri.*

Luzianne Coffee sample tin. Wm. B. Reilly & Company, Inc., New Orleans. *Courtesy of Holt's Country Store, Grandview, Missouri.*

Lithographed four-pound tin pail for Mammy's Favorite Brand Coffee, C.D. Kenny Co., Baltimore, Maryland. *Courtesy of Holt's Country Store, Grandview, Missouri.*

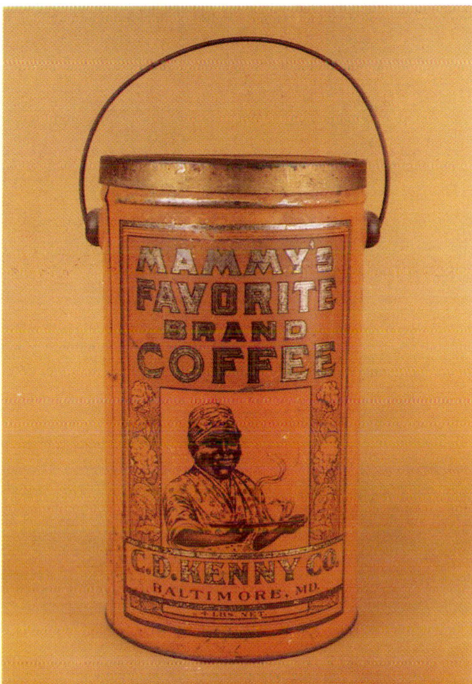

Duncan's Admiration coffee tin. The banner at the bottom proclaims that Duncan is a member of the NRA (National Rifle Association), "We do our part." *Courtesy of Holt's Country Store, Grandview, Missouri.*

Food Products

"Honey, dat's all!" ten-pound tin pail with paper label. Albert & Edith Neidholdt, Brunswick, Missouri. *Courtesy of Holt's Country Store, Grandview, Missouri.*

Longwood Plantation's Pure Cane Syrup tin pail with paper label. S.J. Gianelloni, Jr., Longwood Plantation, East Baton Rouge Parish, Baton Rouge, Louisiana. 6" tall. *Courtesy of Bunny Walker.*

Aunt Dinah molasses, Penick & Ford, Ltd., Inc., New Orleans, Louisiana. *Courtesy of Holt's Country Store, Grandview, Missouri.*

Five gallon Aunt Jemima Cooking and Salad Oil tin with pouring cap. Made at Aunt Jemima Mills, St. Joseph, Missouri, by The Quaker Oats Company, ca. 1935. *Courtesy of Holt's Country Store, Grandview, Missouri.*

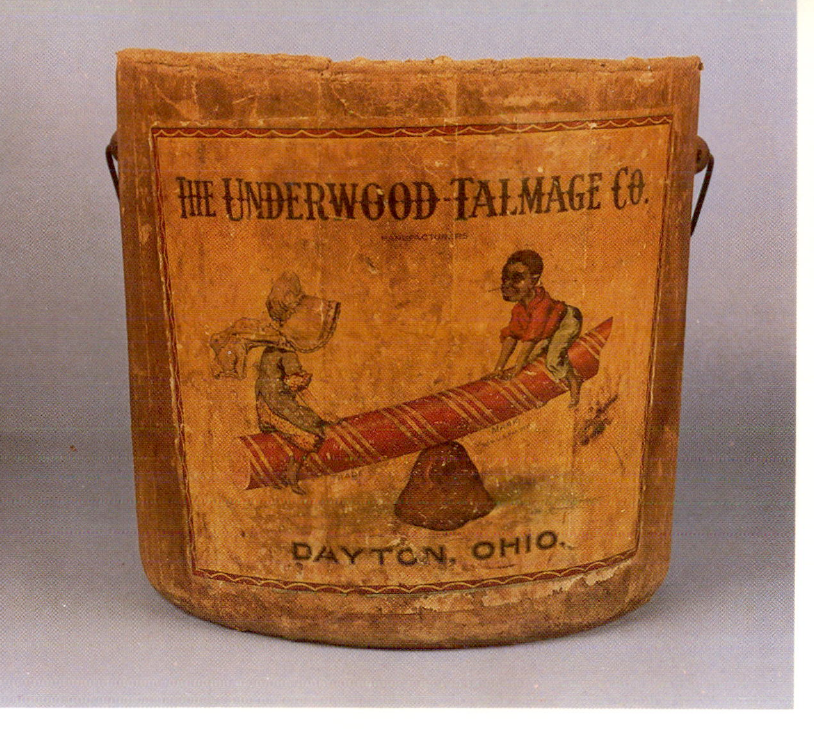

Cardboard candy bucket, The Underwood Talmage Co., Dayton, Ohio. The black and white child on the candy stick teeter-totter was the company trademark. *Courtesy of Holt's Country Store, Grandview, Missouri.*

Pepper tin with paper label for Zanzibar brand ground black pepper featuring native women. B. Heller & Company, Chicago, Illinois, 1927. 9″ x 4.5″ x 4.5″. *Courtesy of The Bookshelf.*

Clear glass beverage bottle from the Mammy Beverage Co., 14″ tall. *Courtesy of Jan Lindenberger, Black By Popular Demand, Colorado Springs, Colorado.*

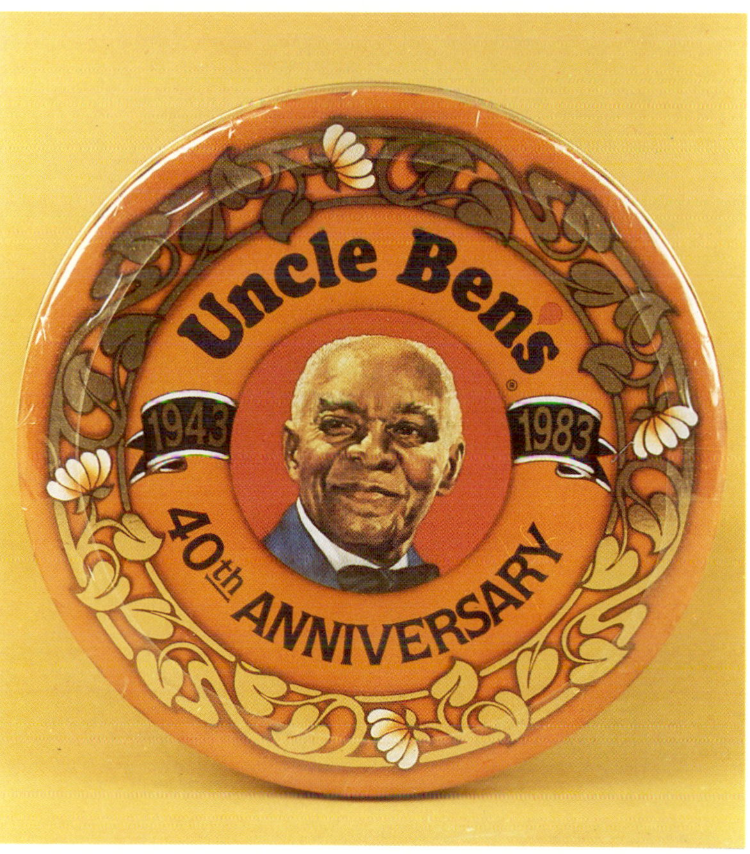

Lithographed tin tray commemorating the fortieth anniversary of Uncle Ben's rice. 1983. *Courtesy of Holt's Country Store, Grandview, Missouri.*

Sunny South Sweet Milk Chocolate Peanuts lithographed tin. *Courtesy of Holt's Country Store, Grandview, Missouri.*

Tobacco

As the word "nigger" became less acceptable in society, the name of this tobacco was changed from "Niggerhair" to "Biggerhair." While the image on the tin remained the same it was labeled as a "Figi Islander" on the later container. The canister on the left is lithographed tin,and the one on the right has a paper label and cardboard top. 6.5" high x 5.5" wide. *Courtesy of The Bookshelf.*

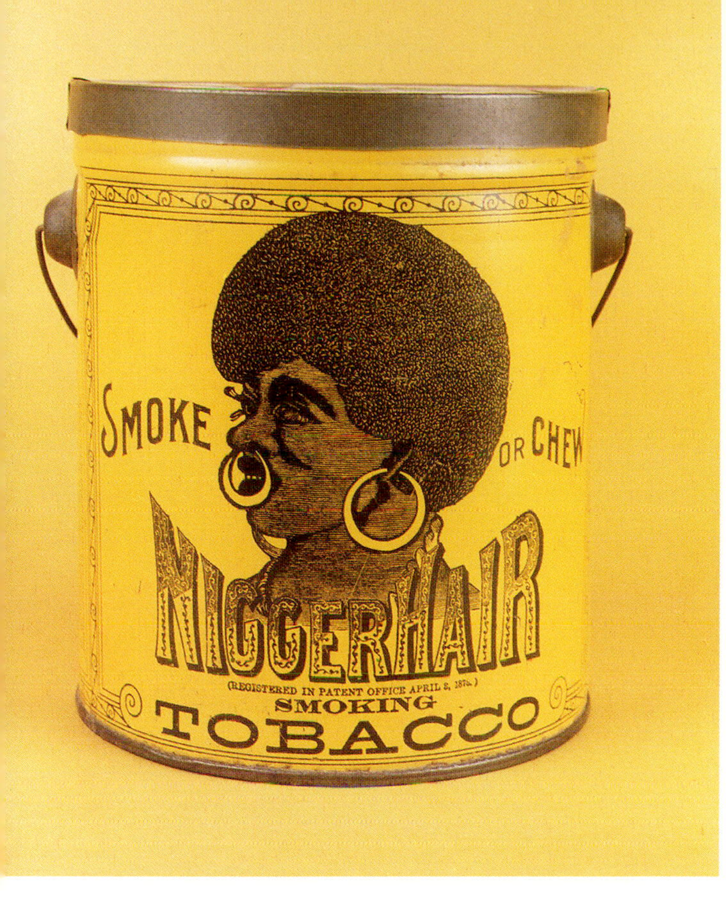

Yellow Niggerhair lithographed tobacco pail. *Courtesy of Holt's Country Store, Grandview, Missouri.*

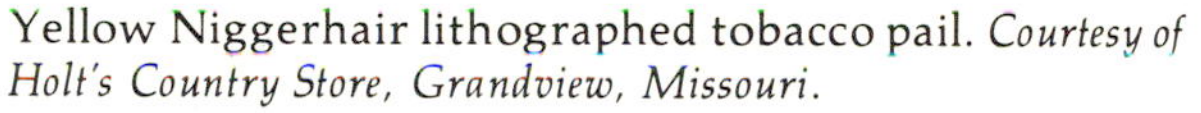

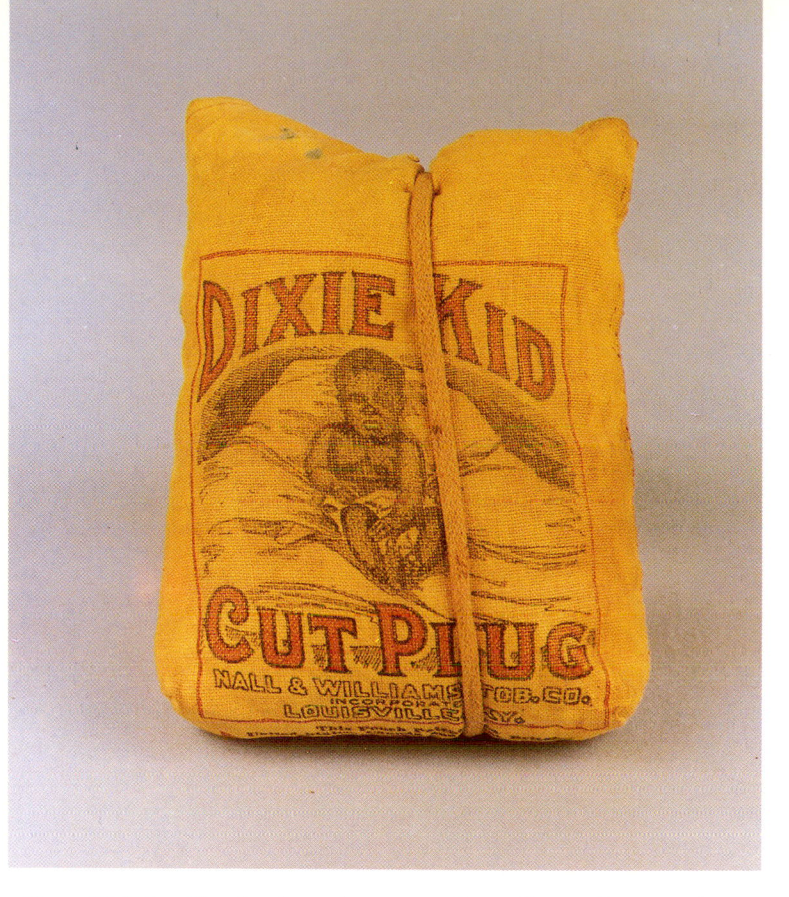

Dixie Kid Cut Plug burlap tobacco pouch, Nall & Williams Tobacco Co., Louisville, Kentucky. *Courtesy of Holt's Country Store, Grandview, Missouri.*

Roly-poly mammy tobacco tin for Mayo Tobacco. *Courtesy of Holt's Country Store, Grandview, Missouri.*

Three Black Kids cigar box for store display. Wood and wood and paper. *Courtesy of Holt's Country Store, Grandview, Missouri.*

Four color lithographed Three Black Kids cigar box, wood and paper. Manufactured by Charles Gross and Company, Philadelphia, Pennsylvania. *Courtesy of Holt's Country Store, Grandview, Missouri.*

Hambone Sweets, 5-cent cigar box, wood and paper. *Courtesy of Holt's Country Store, Grandview, Missouri.*

Davenport Big Head tobacco box. Aug. H. Sunderbruch Cigar Company, Davenport, Iowa, ca. 1910. *Courtesy of Holt's Country Store, Grandview, Missouri.*

Cabin Home tobacco, Neuman & Dinglinger, New York. Trademark by Frey Bros., New York. When closed the cigar box is in the shape of a cabin. Wood and paper. *Courtesy of Holt's Country Store, Grandview, Missouri.*

Temptation cigar box. "These cigars are made of the choicest tobaccos grown on the plantation in the celebrate Vuelta Abajo district of Cuba." Manufactured by the American Cigar Co., Westfield, Massachusetts. The Temptation trademark was transferred from Ghio and Rovira in March, 1898. *Courtesy of Holt's Country Store, Grandview, Missouri.*

Bixby's "Satinola" shoe polish tin. *Courtesy of Holt's Country Store, Grandview, Missouri.*

Lithographed Diamond Match Company tin matchsafe. On the top is a comic scene with the caption "Their first box of drawing room matches. Paterfamilias: You chillun keep back deah! You want you' heads blowed off'n you' shouldas?." *Courtesy of Holt's Country Store, Grandview, Missouri.*

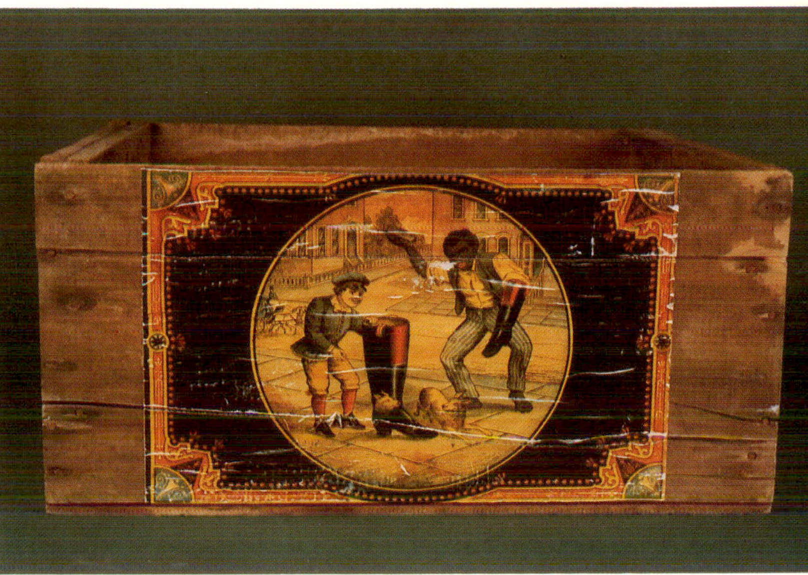

Wooden crate for Mason's Challenge Blacking for boots. Paper label. *Courtesy of Elizabeth Holt and Scott Lofquist.*

Wooden display case for Mason's Challenge Blacking, which held three dozen tins. Lithographed paper label. *Courtesy of Holt's Country Store, Grandview, Missouri.*

Lithographed tin of Mason's Original Challenge Blacking. Jas. S. Mason, Inc., established 1892, Philadelphia, Pennsylvania. *Courtesy of Holt's Country Store, Grandview, Missouri.*

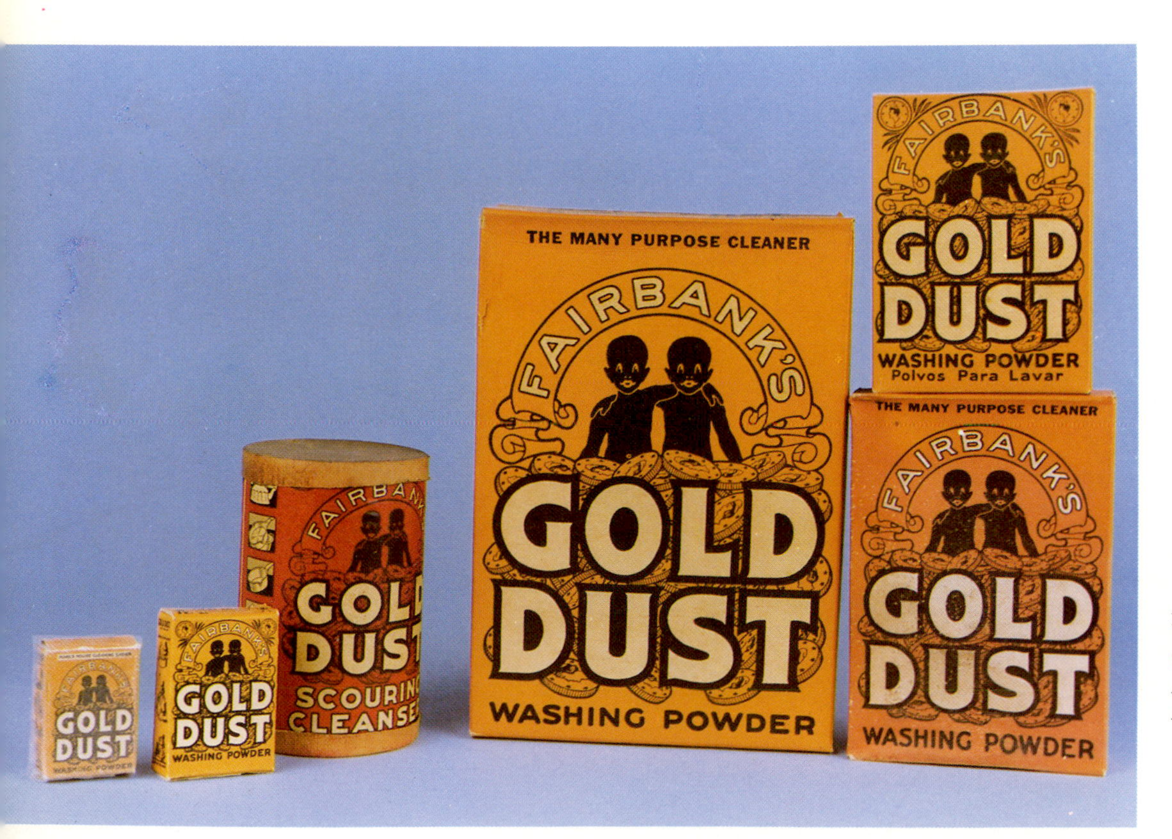

A variety of Gold Dust Washing Powder containers. S.K. Fairbanks. *Courtesy of Holt's Country Store, Grandview, Missouri.*

Box of Sharpoint Wire Cobbler Nails, paper. *Courtesy of Holt's Country Store, Grandview, Missouri.*

Fun-to-Wash Washing Powder, manufactured by the Hygienic Laboratories, Buffalo, NY. *Courtesy of Holt's country Store, Grandview, Missouri.*

Crate for Colburns Bag Blue. Wood with paper label. *Courtesy of Holt's Country Store, Grandview, Missouri.*

Die-cut Gold Dust figure. *Courtesy of Holt's Country Store, Grandview, Missouri.*

Dickey's White Side Wall Tire Cleaner. *Courtesy of Holt's Country Store, Grandview, Missouri.*

Dinah Black Enamel, a paint for use on stoves, fences, gears and other surfaces. *Courtesy of Holt's Country Store, Grandview, Missouri.*

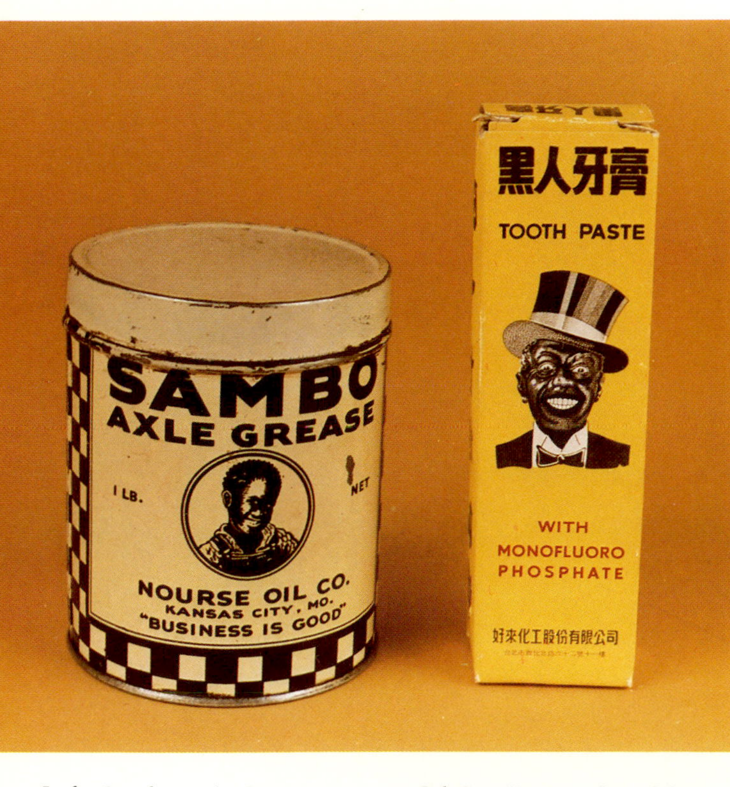

Left: Sambo Axle Grease, Nourse Oil Co., Kansas City, Missouri; right: a toothpaste manufactured in Japan. *Courtesy of Holt's Country Store, Grandview, Missouri.*

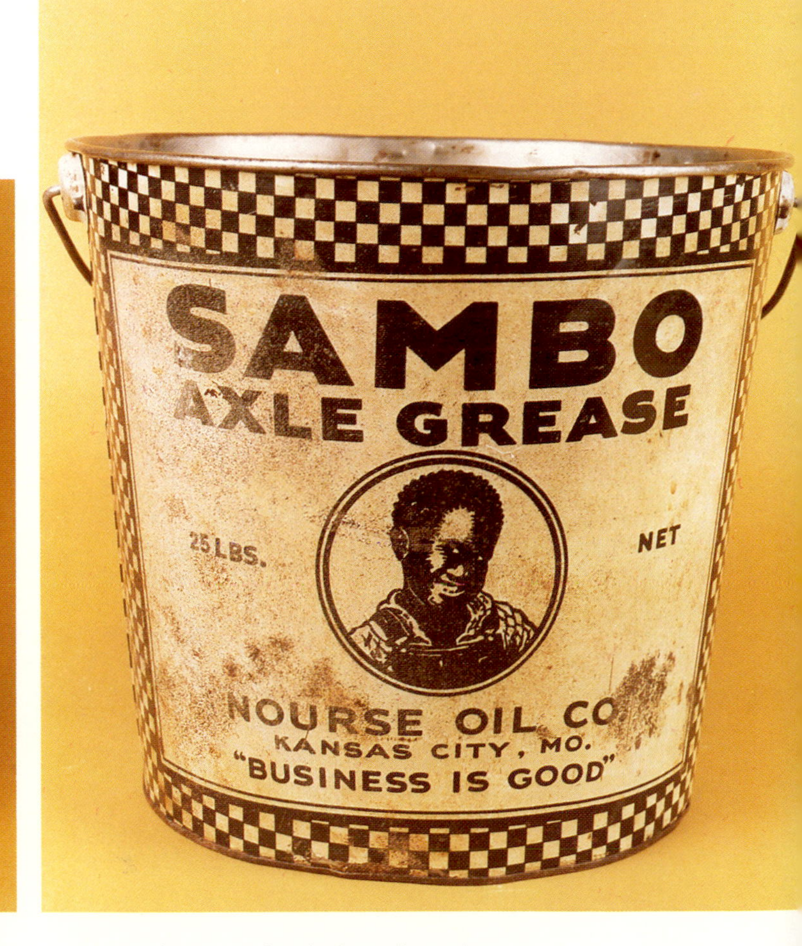

Twenty-five pound pail of Sambo Axle Grease, Nourse Oil Co., Kansas City, Missouri. *Courtesy of Holt's Country Store, Grandview, Missouri.*

Carter's Inky Racer, Carter's Ink Co., Boston. A two-step method for erasing ink writing or stains involved using the solution in bottle one (on the right), blotting it, and then using solution number two. It was suggested that only one or two letters be erased at a time. *Courtesy of Holt's Country Store, Grandview, Missouri.*

Lithographed biscuit tin from the Southern Biscuit Co., Richmond, Virginia. The company slogan was "Southern cakes for Southern tastes." *Courtesy of Holt's Country Store, Grandview, Missouri.*

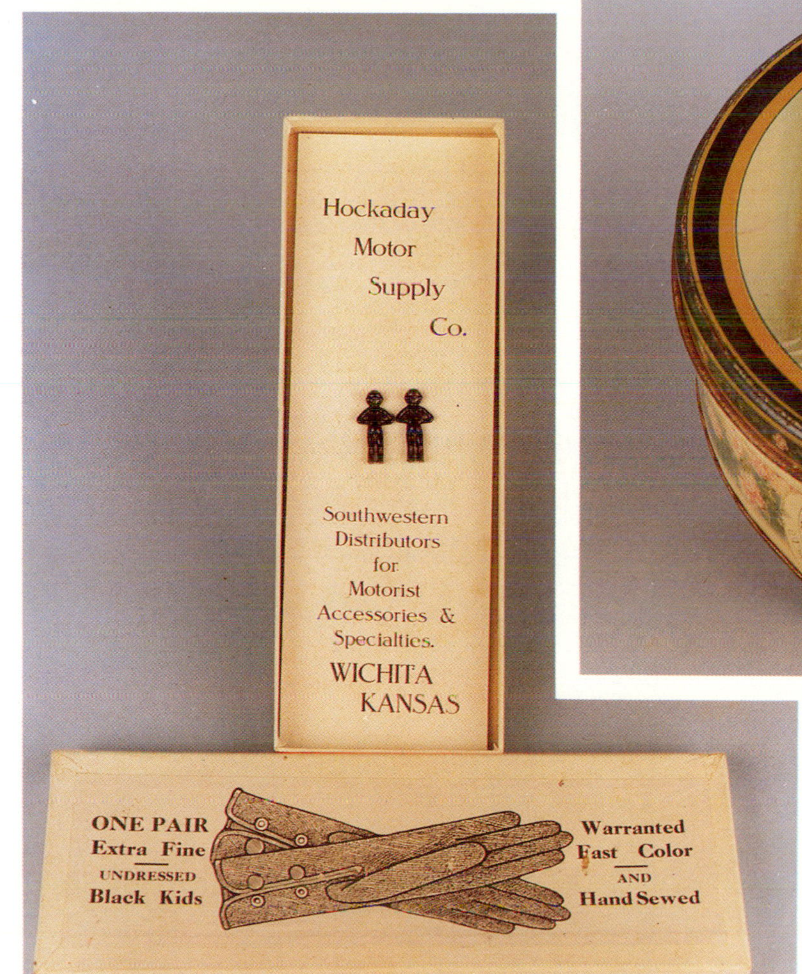

A humorous advertising piece offered "One pair, extra fine, undressed black kids" on the cover of the box, with a picture of fine gloves. Inside the box are two frozen Charlotte bisque undressed black dolls and an advertisement for Hockaday Motor Supply Co., Wichita, Kansas. *Courtesy of Holt's Country Store, Grandview, Missouri.*

Music

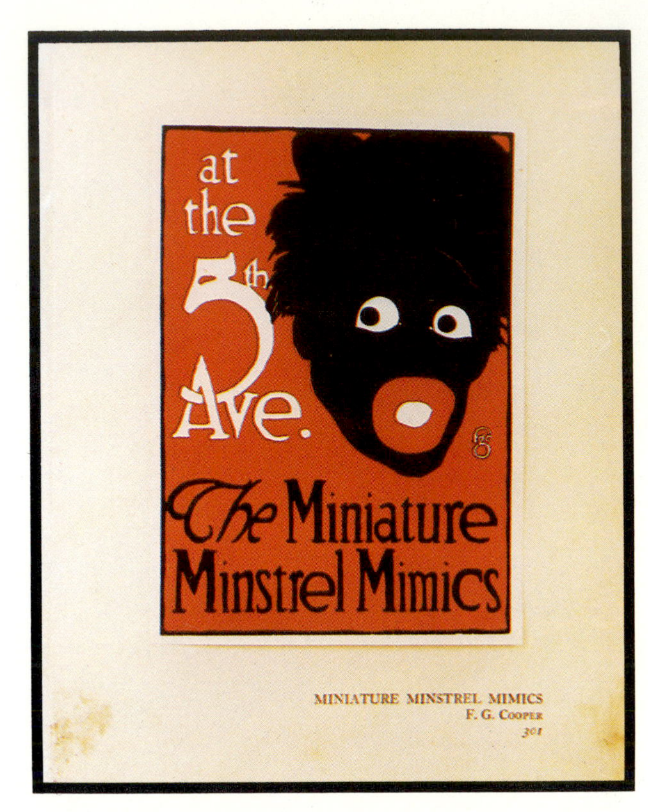

Poster for the Miniature Minstrel Mimics, at the 5th Avenue Theatre, by F.G. Cooper. *Courtesy of Elizabeth Holt and Scott Lofquist.*

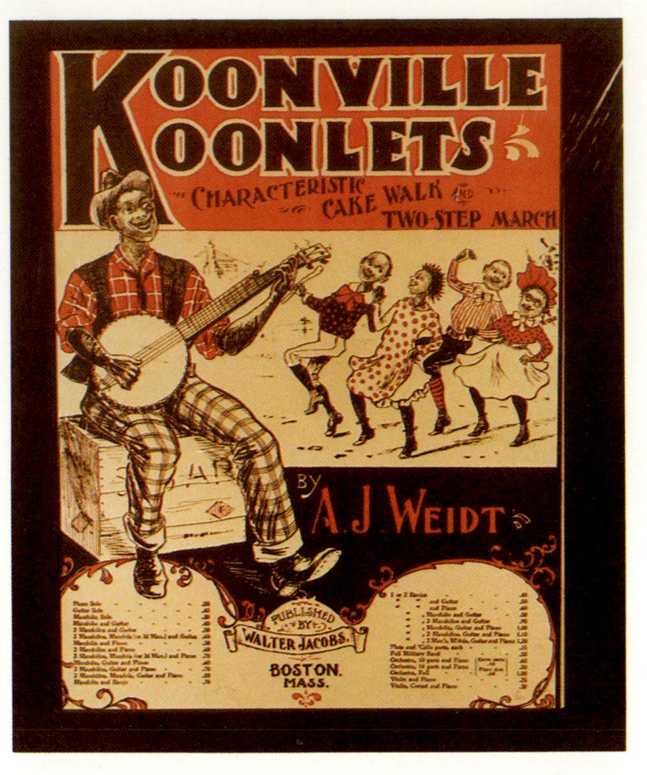

"Koonville Koonlets" sheet music by A.J. Weidt. Published by Walter Jacobs, Boston, Massachusetts. *Courtesy of Elizabeth Holt and Scott Lofquist.*

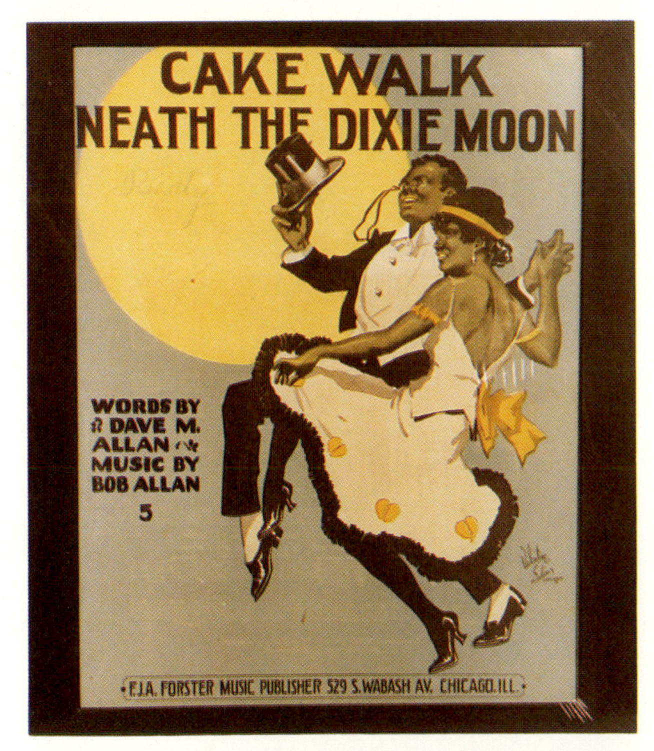

"Cake Walk Neath the Dixie Moon" sheet music by Dave M. Allan and Bob Allan. Published by F.J.A. Forster Music, Chicago, Illinois. The cover design, featuring less stereotyped characters, is by Valentine Dulim, Chicago. *Courtesy of Elizabeth Holt and Scott Lofquist.*

"Chocolate Creams" sheet music by Will F. Burke. Published by Vandersloot Music Co., Williamsport, Pennsylvania. *Courtesy of Elizabeth Holt and Scott Lofquist.*

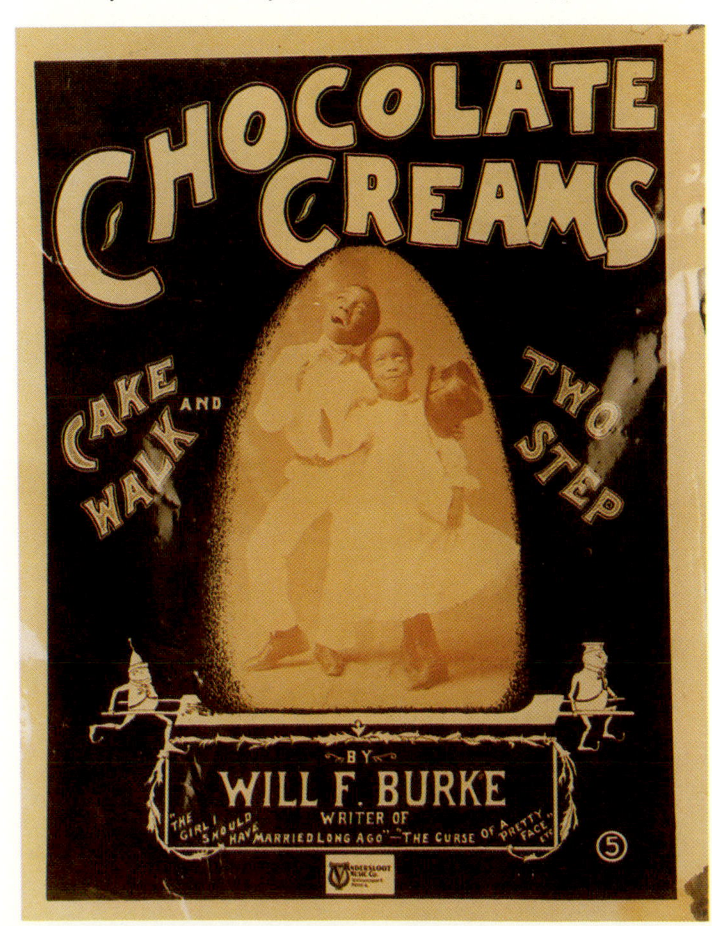

"I Don't Care What Happens to Me Now" by Artie Hall, "the original Georgia Coon Shouter." Published by Whitney-Warner Publishing Company, Detroit, Michigan. *Courtesy of Elizabeth Holt and Scott Lofquist.*

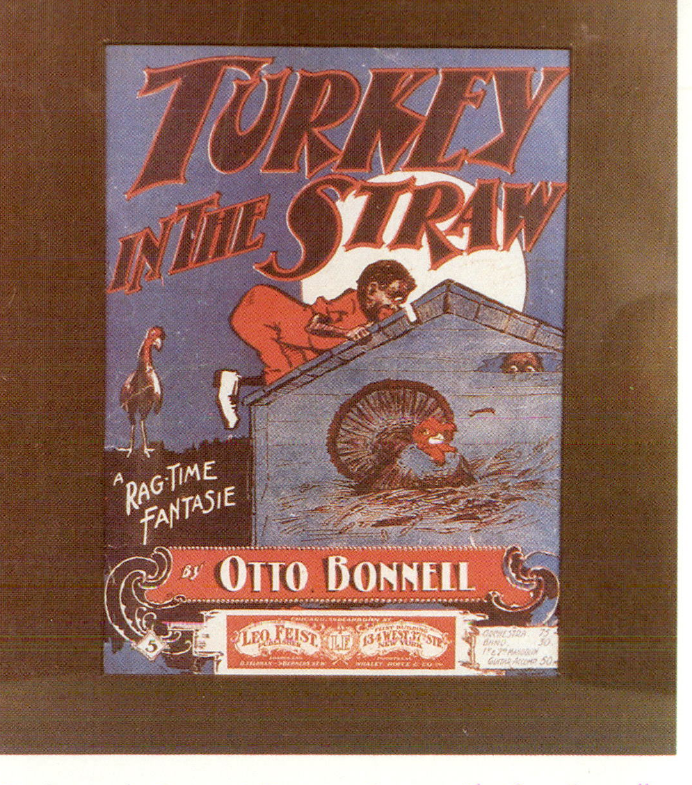

"Turkey in the Straw, A Rag-time Fantasie" by Otto Bonnell. Published by Leo. Feist, New York. *Courtesy of Elizabeth Holt and Scott Lofquist.*

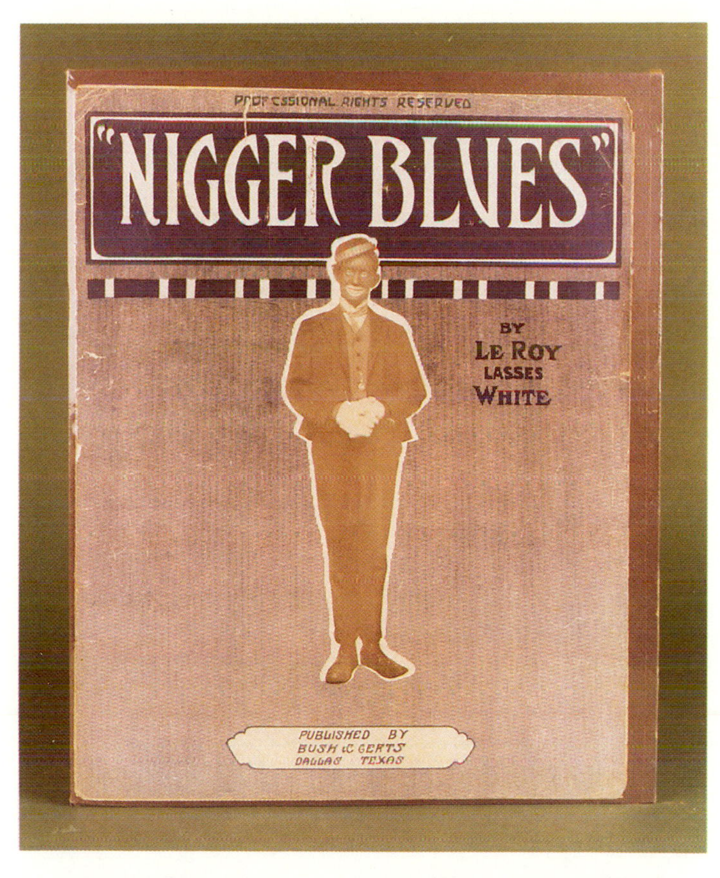

"Nigger Blues" by Leroy Lasses White (presumably the cover photo is of Mr. White in blackface). Published by Bush & Gerts, Dallas, Texas, 1908. *Courtesy of Elizabeth Holt and Scott Lofquist.*

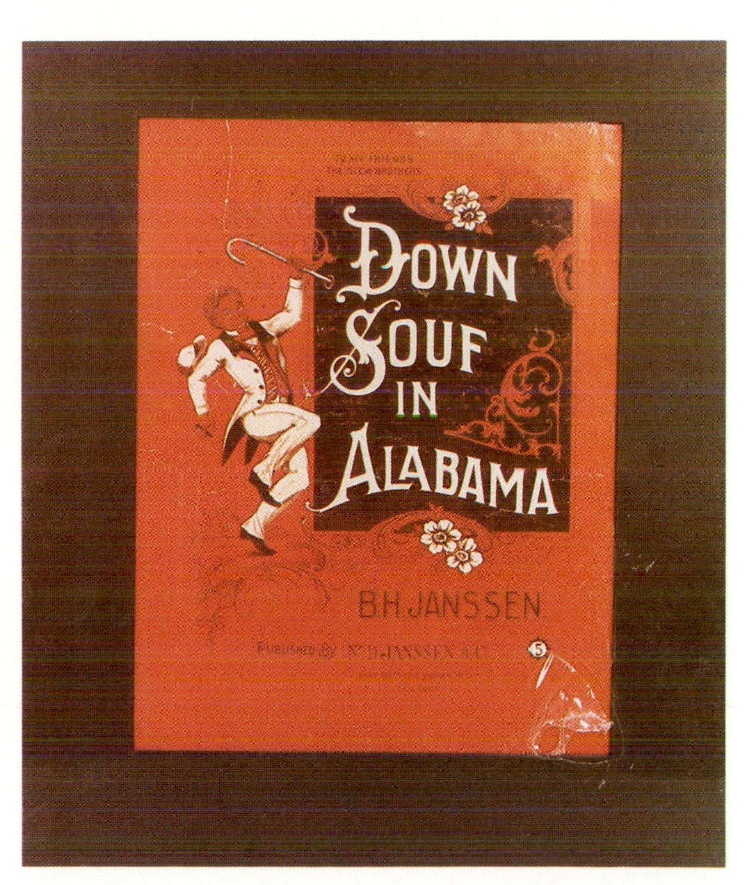

"Down Souf in Alabama" by B.H. Janssen. Published by M.D. Janssen & Co., New York. *Courtesy of Elizabeth Holt and Scott Lofquist.*

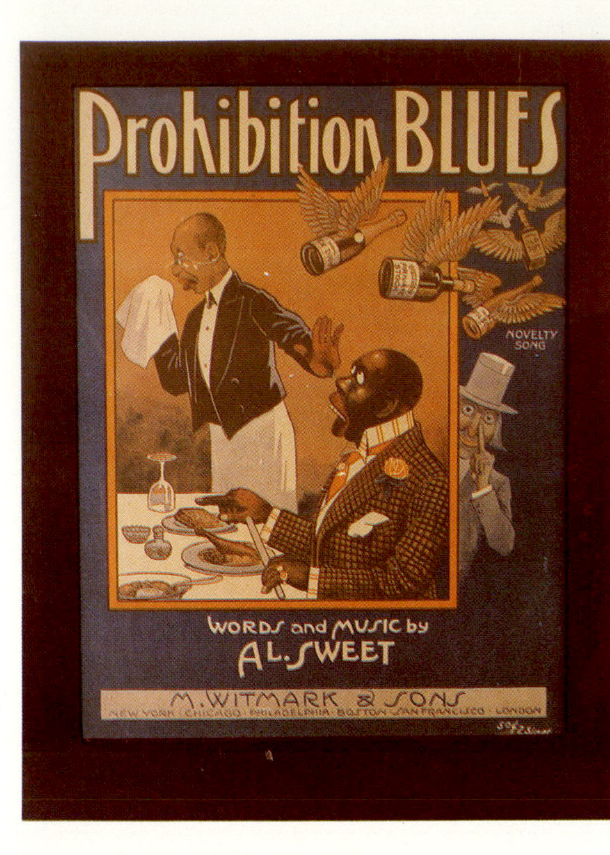

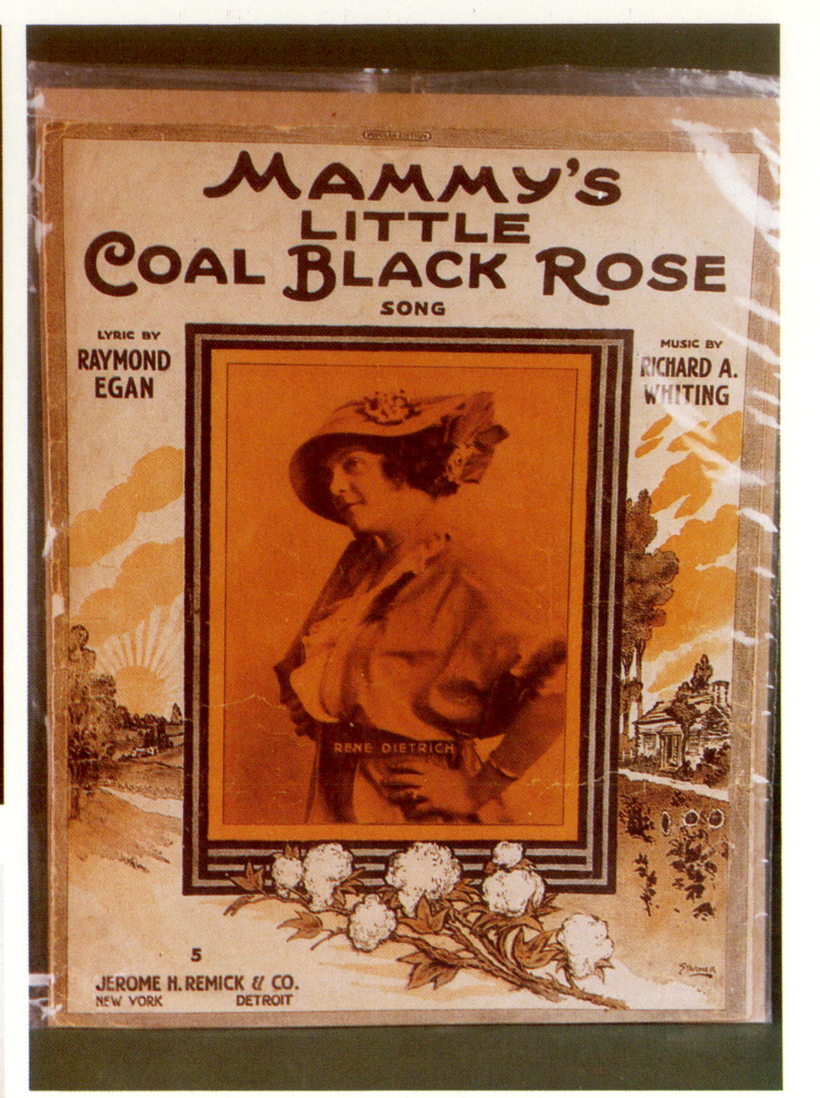

Top left:
"Prohibition Blues" by Al. Sweet. Published by M. Witmark & Sons, New York. *Courtesy of Elizabeth Holt and Scott Lofquist.*

Top right:
"Mammy's Little Coal Black Rose," music by Richard A. Whiting, words by Raymond Egan. Published by Jerome H. Remick & Co., New York. Cover design by Starmer. *Courtesy of Elizabeth Holt and Scott Lofquist.*

Bottom left:
"Coon, Coon, Coon," music by Leo Friedman, words by Gene Jefferson. Introduced and sung by Lew Dockstader, it apparently was also in the repertoire of Dorothy Morton. Published by Sol Bloom, Chicago, ca. 1901. Cover design by Igor Keller. *Courtesy of Elizabeth Holt and Scott Lofquist.*

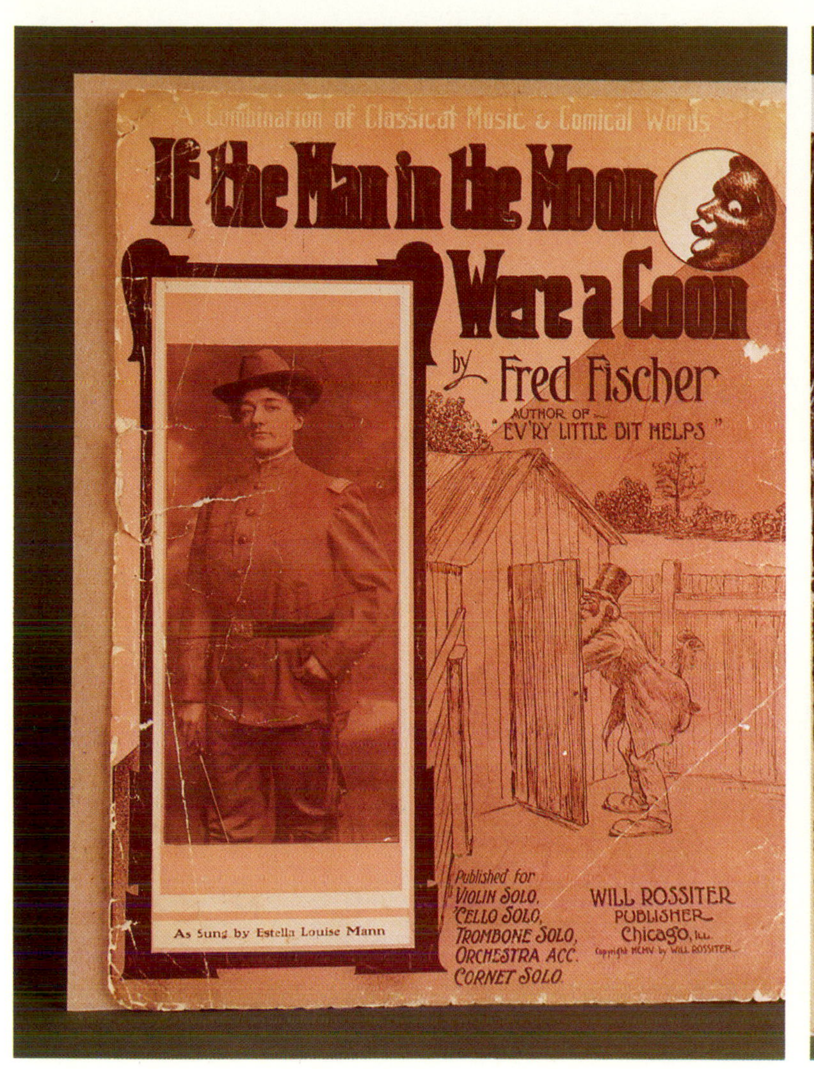

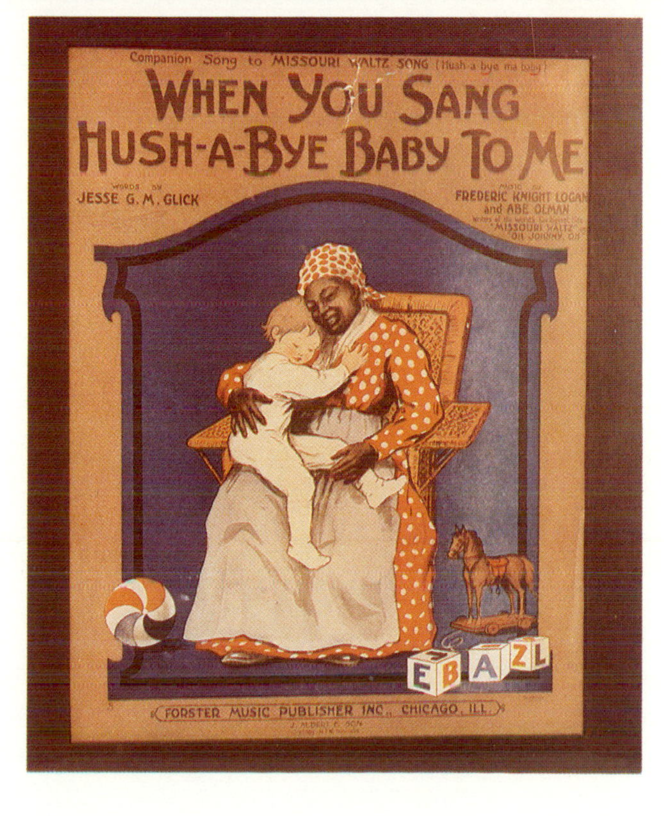

Top left:
"If the Man in the Moon Were a Coon—A Combination of Classical Music & Comical Words" by Fred Fischer. The photo is apparently of Estella Louise Mann, though the military outfit is confusing. Published by Will Rossiter Publisher, Chicago, Illinois, copyright 1905. *Courtesy of Elizabeth Holt and Scott Lofquist.*

Top right:
"Rastus Rag" by H.A. Fischler. Published by Vandersloot Music Publishing Co., Williamsport, Pennsylvania. Cover art by W. J. Dittmar. *Courtesy of Elizabeth Holt and Scott Lofquist.*

Bottom right:
"When You Sang Hush-A-Bye Baby to Me," music by Frederic Knight Logan and Abe Olman, words by Jesse G. M. Glick. Published by Forster Music Publisher Inc., Chicago. Cover design by Starmer. *Courtesy of Elizabeth Holt and Scott Lofquist.*

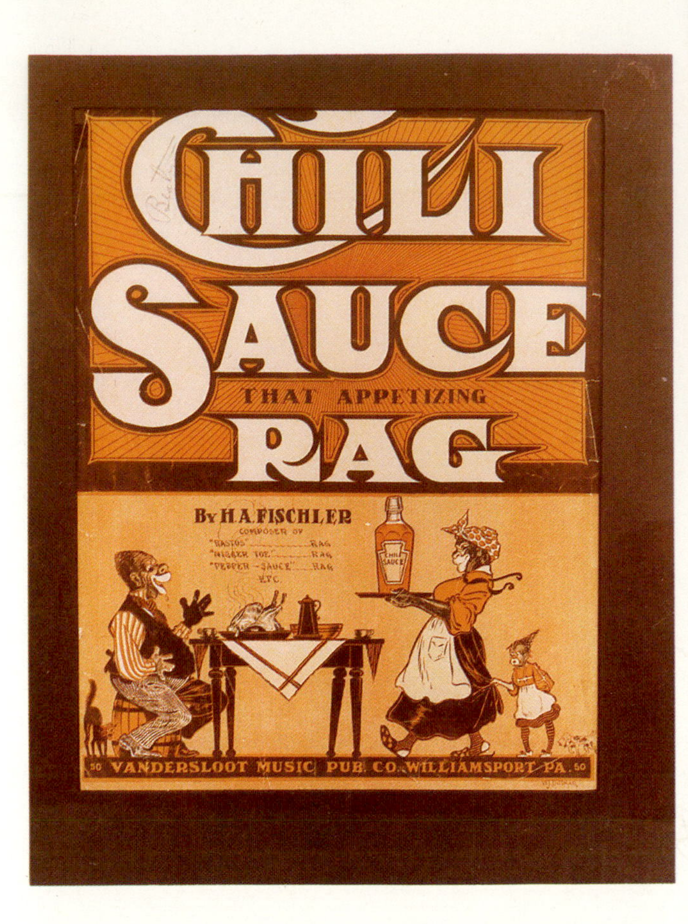

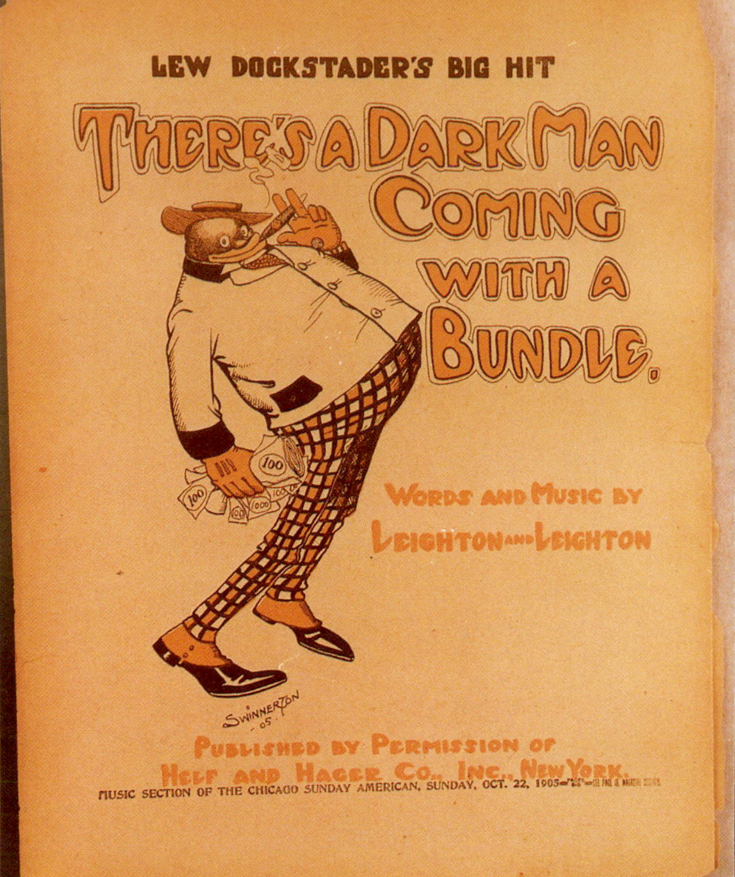

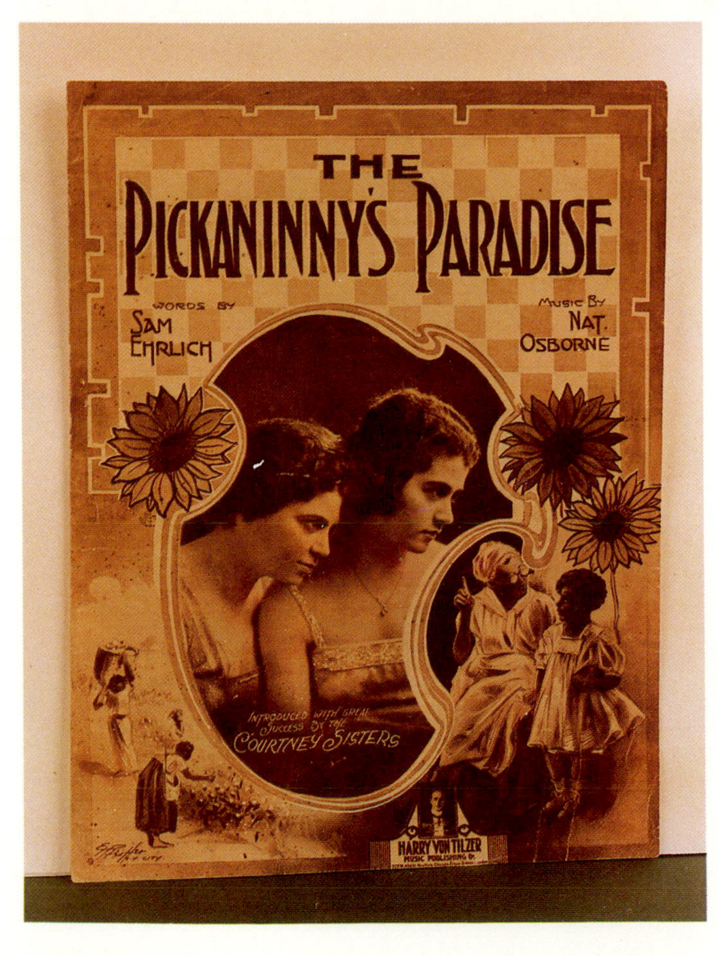

Top left:
"Chili Sauce-That Appetizing Rag" by H.A. Fischler. Published by Vandersloot Music Publishing Company, Williamsport, Pennsylvania. Cover art by W. J. Dittmar. *Courtesy of Elizabeth Holt and Scott Lofquist.*

Top right:
"There's a Dark Man Coming with a Bundle" by Leighton and Leighton. As often happened this piece was published in the Music Section of the Chicago Sunday American, October 22, 1905, with permission of Helf and Hager Co., Inc., New York. The art work is by Swinnerton. *Courtesy of Elizabeth Holt and Scott Lofquist.*

Bottom left:
"The Pickaninny's Paradise," music by Nat Osborne, words by Sam Ehrlich. "Sung with great success by the Courtney Sisters," pictured. Published by Harry Von Tilzer Music Publishing Co., New York. Cover art by E.P. Feiffer (?), New York. *Courtesy of Elizabeth Holt and Scott Lofquist.*

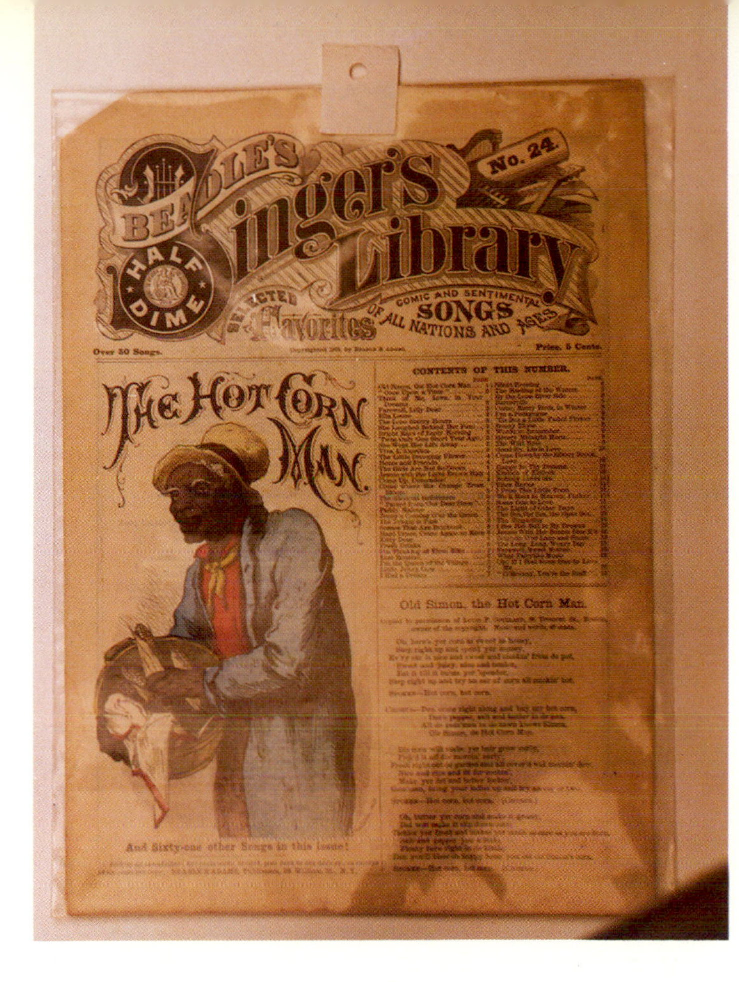

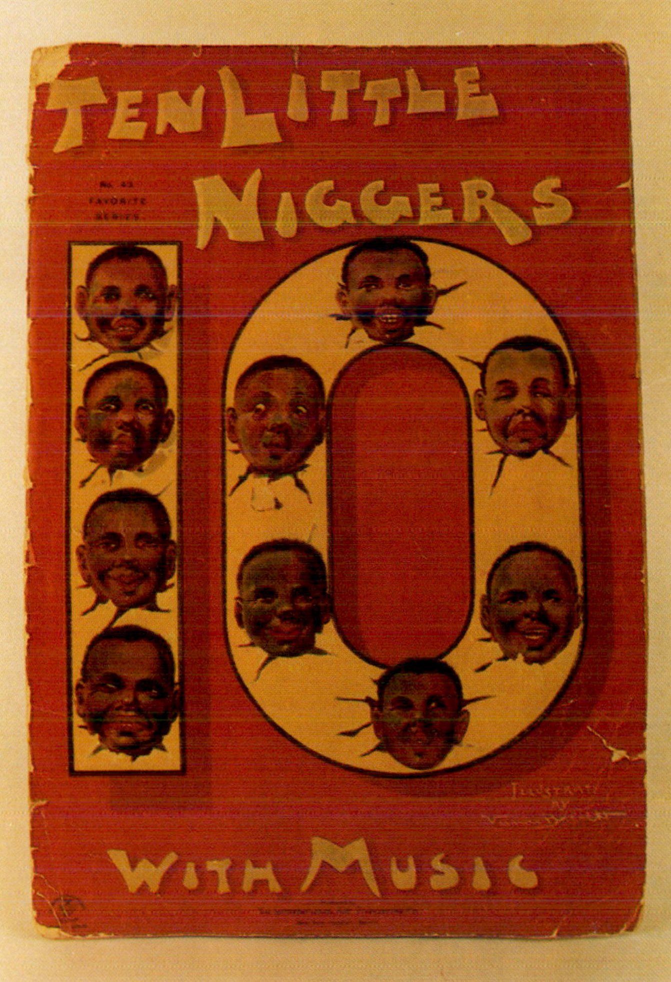

Top left:
"Beadle's Singer's Library" was a periodical in the late nineteenth century specializing in "Comic and sentimental songs of all nations and ages." Issue No. 24 features the song "The Hot Corn Man," copyrighted by Louis P. Goullaud, Boston. The "Singer's Library" was published by Beadle & Adams Publishers, New York. Copyright 1878. *Courtesy of a private collection.*

Top right:
"Beadle's Singers Library-No. 40", 1879 featuring "Tis but a Little Faded Flower." The song was used with permission of Firth, Pond & Company, New York. *Courtesy of a private collection.*

Bottom right:
"Ten Little Niggers" from the Favorite Series of the International Art Publishing Company, New York. This music book was illustrated by Vernon Barrett. *Courtesy of Holt's Country Store, Grandview, Missouri.*

The first pages of "Ten Little Niggers" from McLoughlin Bros. *Courtesy of Fran and Jim Pohrer.*

"Ten Little Niggers" from the BoPeep Series of McLoughlin Bros., New York, ca. 1875. *Courtesy of Fran and Jim Pohrer.*

Golliwoggs

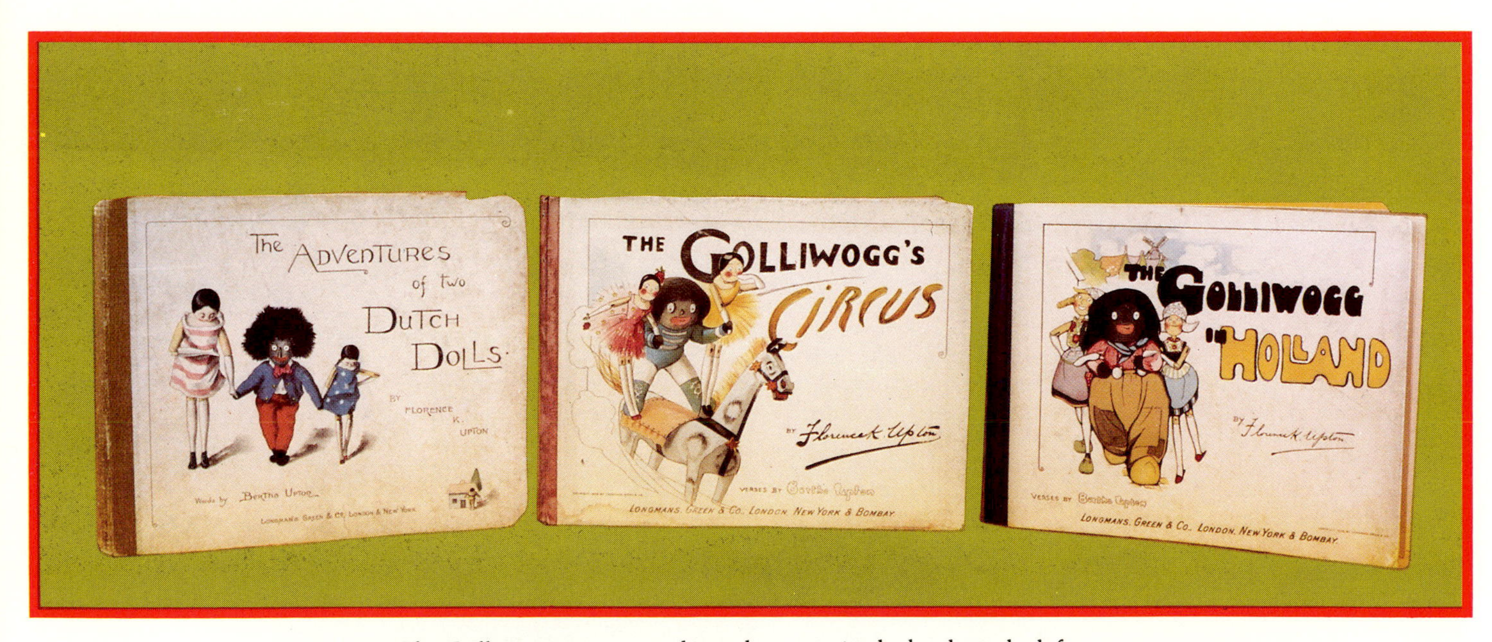

The Golliwogg was created as a character in the book on the left, *The Adventures of the Dutch Dolls*, illustrated by Florence K. Upton, with words by Bertha Upton and published by Longmans Green & Company, London in 1895. Later books in the series included *The Golliwogg's Circus* and *The Golliwogg in Holland." Courtesy of Schneider's Antique Toys, Lancaster, Pennsylvania.*

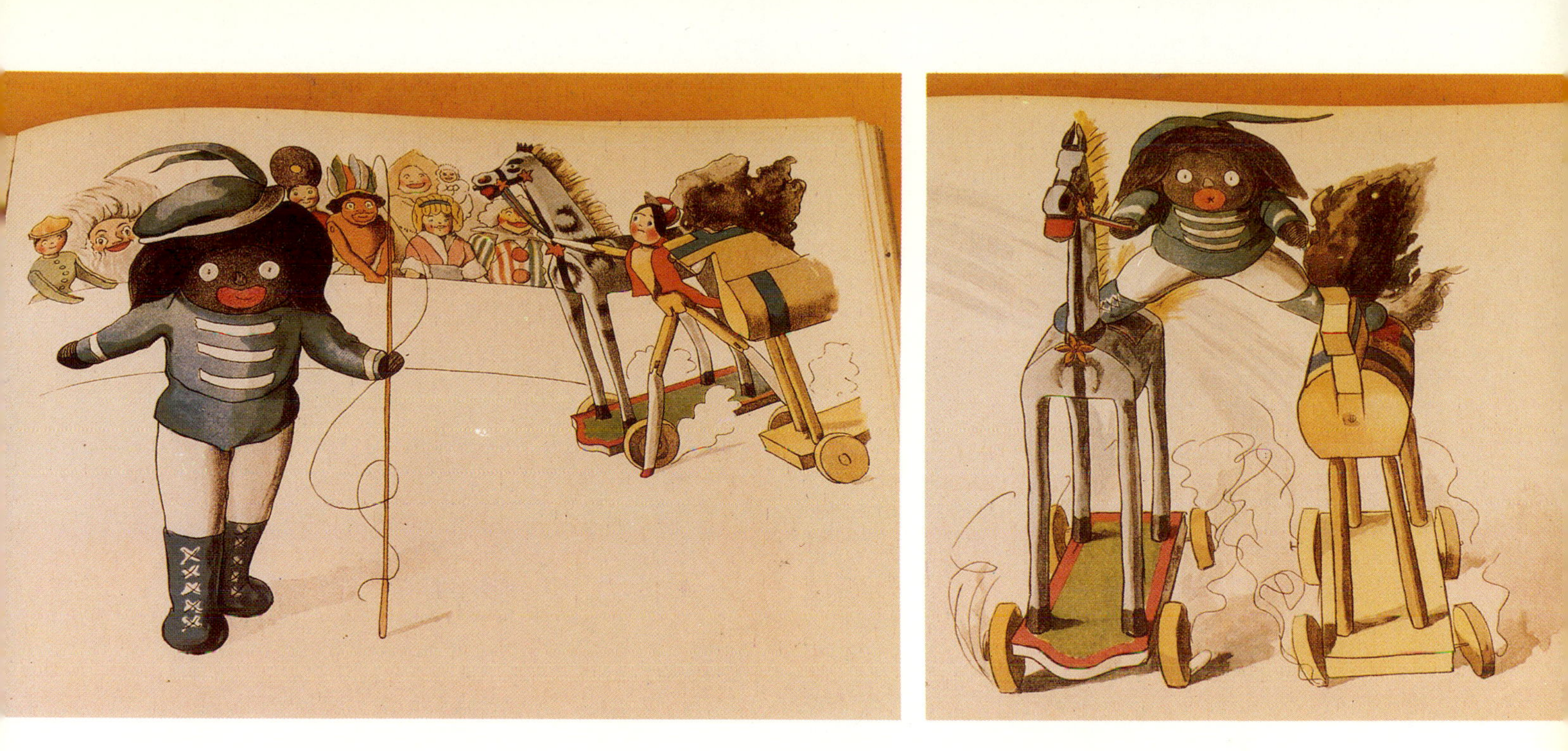

Pages from *The Golliwogg's Circus. Courtesy of Schneider's Antique Toys, Lancaster, Pennsylvania.*

Much of the popularity of the Golliwogg in England is its use as a trademark for Robertson Marmalade. Cardboard die cut figure. Golliwogs are now called "Gollies," the "wog" being considered derogatory. To be legal in England, the images of the Gollies cannot be condescending. James Robertson & Sons. *Courtesy of Bill Harrap, Fun Antiques, Sheffield, England.*

This small enamel pin was offered as a premium from Robertson Marmalade. Inside the cap of the jar were paper Golliwogs which people collected. When they had gathered eight, they would send them in and receive a pin in this series. James Robertson & Sons. *Courtesy of Bill Harrap, Fun Antiques, Sheffield, England.*

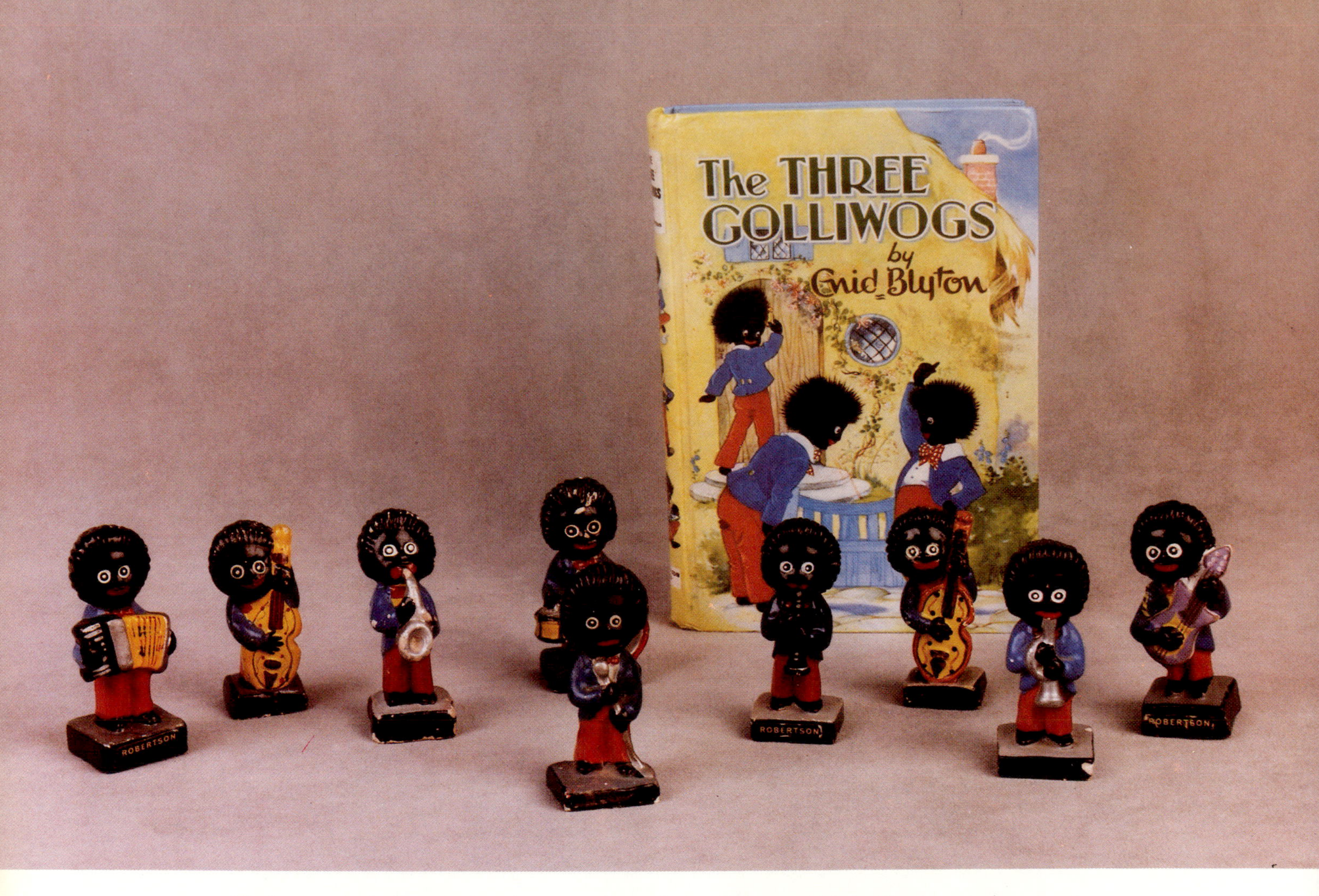

The book in the background is *The Three Golliwogs* by Enid Blyton, published by Dean & Son, London, 1969. The band figures are 3″ high and were given as premiums with Robertson Marmalade by James Robertson & Sons. *Courtesy of Bill Harrap, Fun Antiques, Sheffield, England.*

Golliwogg plate showing the trademark on the reverse. *Courtesy of Bunny Walker.*

Golliwogg still bank, made by John Harper, England, ca. 1925. Cast iron, 6". *Courtesy of Stuart Cropper, Sussex, England.*

Cashew tin, England ca. 1930s. Rountree's Cashous, "Breath Candy Sweets," York, England. 3.25". *Courtesy of John Haley, Halifax, England.*

"The Freshman," a lithograph on paper by Lillian Cheesman, ca. 1920. This image of a white child teaching a black would be considered condescending and no longer permitted in England. *Courtesy of Bill Harrap, Fun Antiques, Sheffield, England.*

Dean's rag dolls, ca. 1930s. 15" high. *Courtesy of Bill Harrap, Fun Antiques, Sheffield, England.*

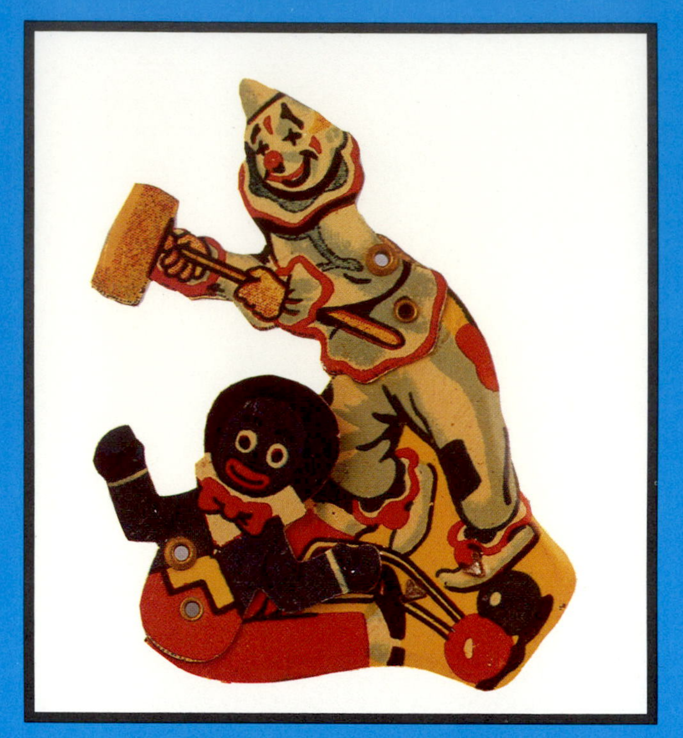

Movable Golliwogg circus figure. *Courtesy of Holt's Country Store, Grandview, Missouri.*

Golliwogg doll from a kit. *Courtesy of Elizabeth Holt and Scott Lofquist.*

Birthday card, 1920s. Golliwoggs are often shown with teddies. 4.25" x 4". *Courtesy of Bill Harrap, Fun Antiques, Sheffield, England.*

Golliwogg perfume bottles. *Courtesy of Holt's Country Store, Grandview, Missouri.*

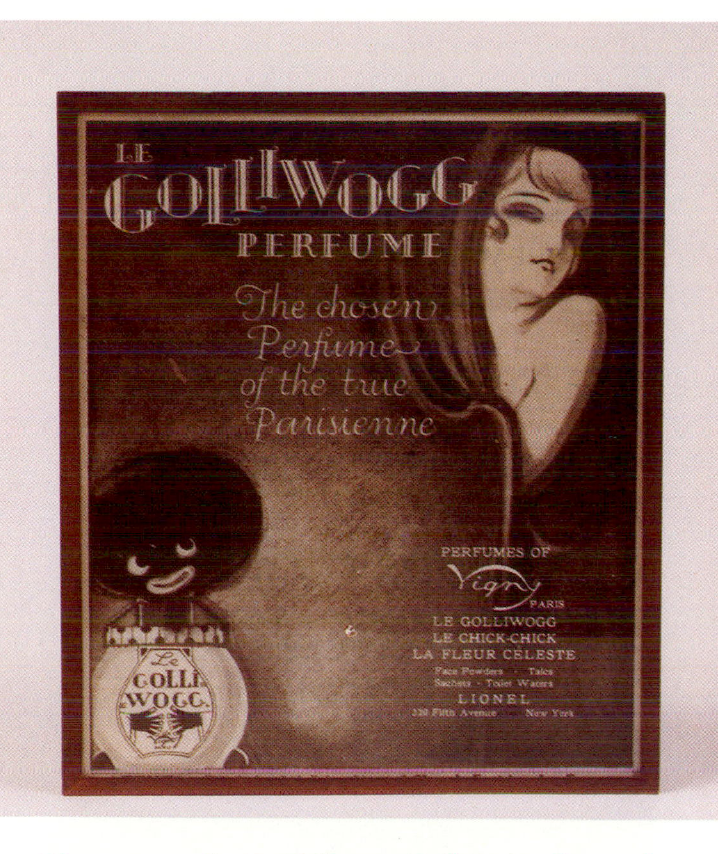

Advertisement for Le Golliwogg Perfume, perfumes of Vigny, Paris at Lionel, New York, 1926. 6" x 5". *Courtesy of Bunny Walker.*

Golliwogg perfume bottle, 4.5" high. *Courtesy of Jan Lindenberger, Black By Popular Demand, Colorado Springs, Colorado.*

Cards

Top left:
A Valentine greeting. *Courtesy of Holt's Country Store, Grandview, Missouri.*

Top right:
A Christmas card. *Courtesy of Jim Morrison.*

Bottom right:
Die-cut valentine card. *Courtesy of Holt's Country Store, Grandview, Missouri.*

Greeting card. "A Buzza Motto," G.L. Salisbury, copyright 1925. *Courtesy of Holt's Country Store, Grandview, Missouri.*

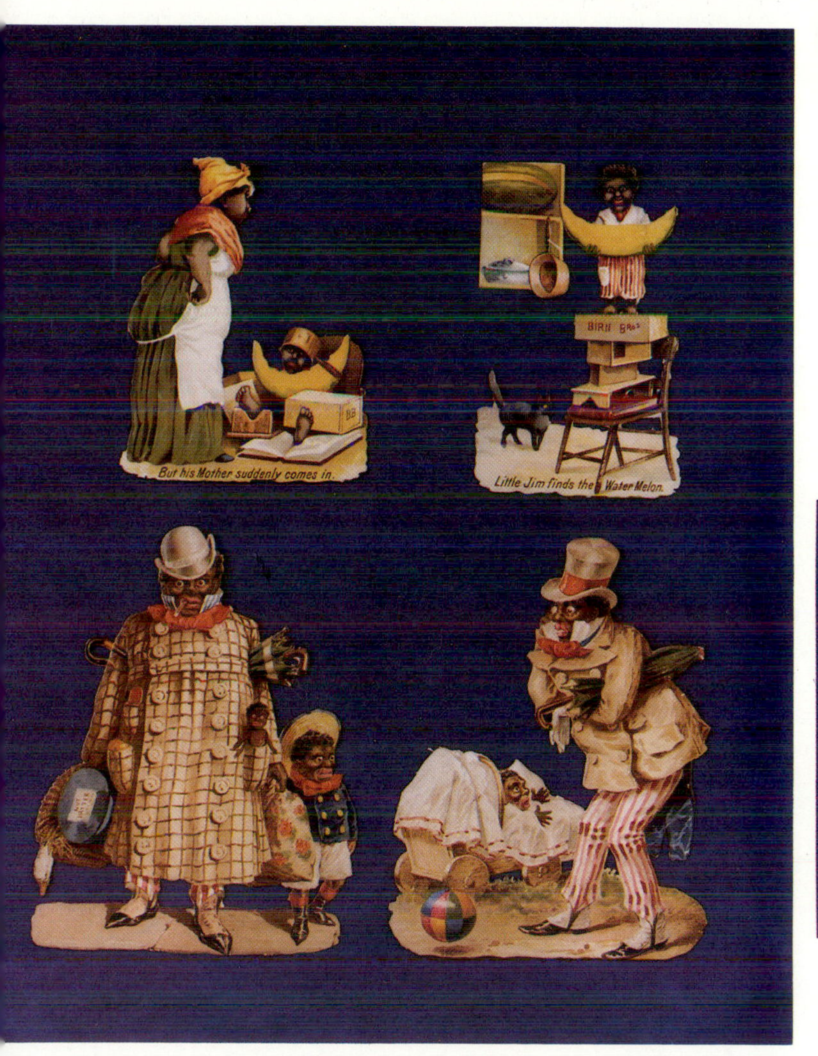

Four die-cut cards. English. *Courtesy of Jim Morrison.*

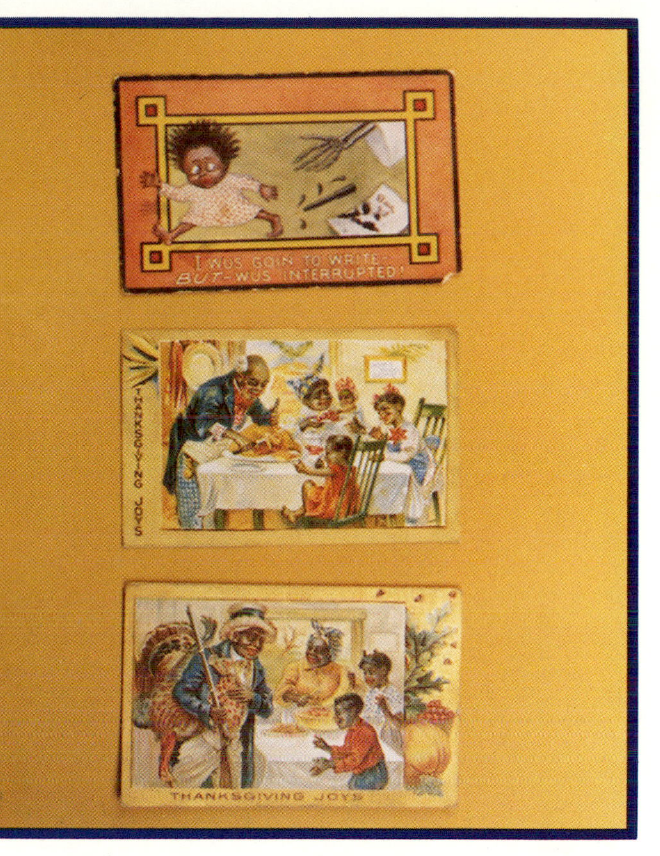

A general greeting card and two Thanksgiving cards. *Courtesy of Holt's Country Store, Grandview, Missouri.*

Movable Christmas and Valentine cards. The flowers in the card on the left move, and the head, tail, and eyes move in the other. *Courtesy of Holt's Country Store, Grandview, Missouri.*

Three minstrel Christmas cards. English. *Courtesy of Jim Morrison.*

(Clockwise from top left): "A Bright New Year;" "When I wish you a happy Christmas, see that you get it;" two of a series of cards featuring the antics of Sambo and the chef, No. 4 "A Christmas of Love," and No. 5 "A Christmas of Peace." The lower right card is signed Ellam and reads "Many be your Xmas joys, and may they last for ever, and ah 'the slings of outrageous fortune' may you meet with never." English. *Courtesy of Jim Morrison.*

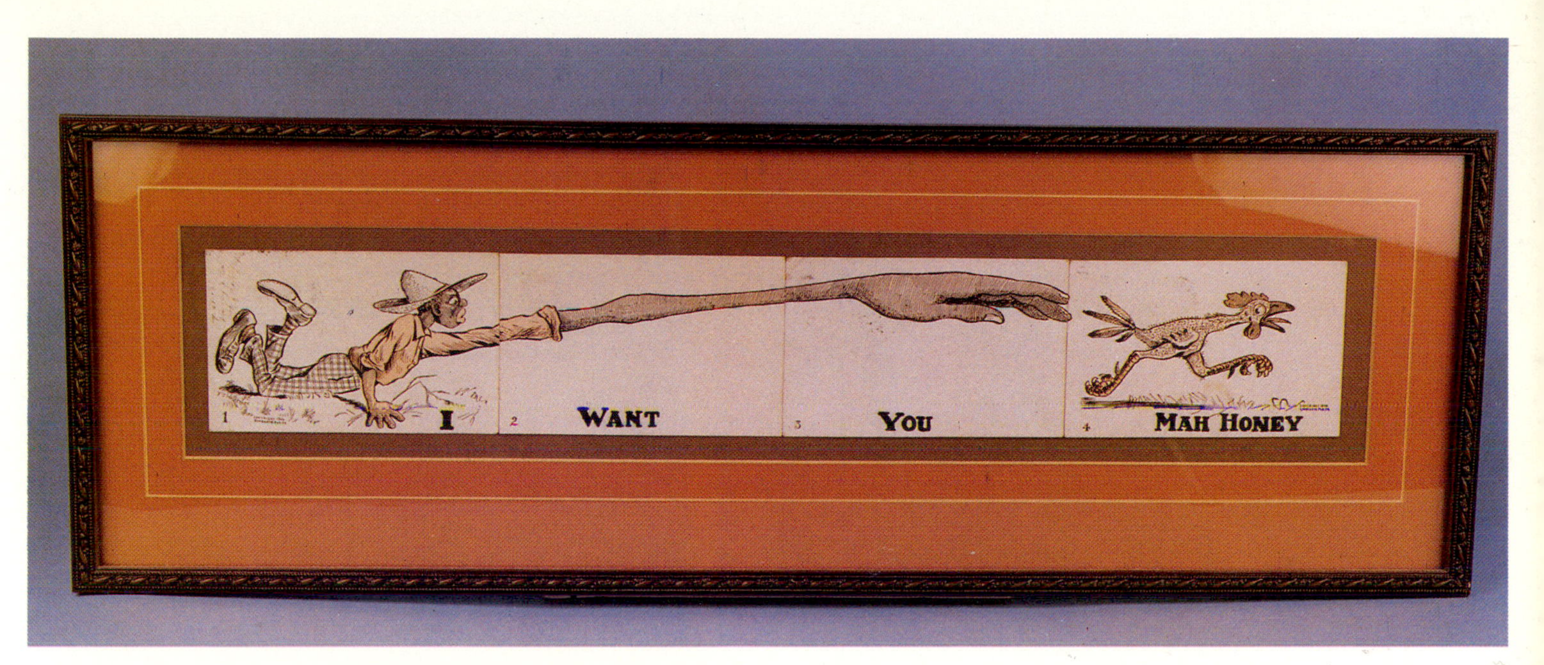

Four rare postcards make up this greeting. Syndicate Publishing Co., copyright 1906. *Courtesy of Holt's Country Store, Grandview, Missouri.*

Sympathy card, Ullman Mfg. Co., New York. Artist initials: M.D.S. *Courtesy of Holt's Country Store, Grandview, Missouri.*

Greeting card, Curt Teich & Co. *Courtesy of Deborah Holt.*

Card with three attached black frozen Charlotte china figures. *Courtesy of a private collection.*

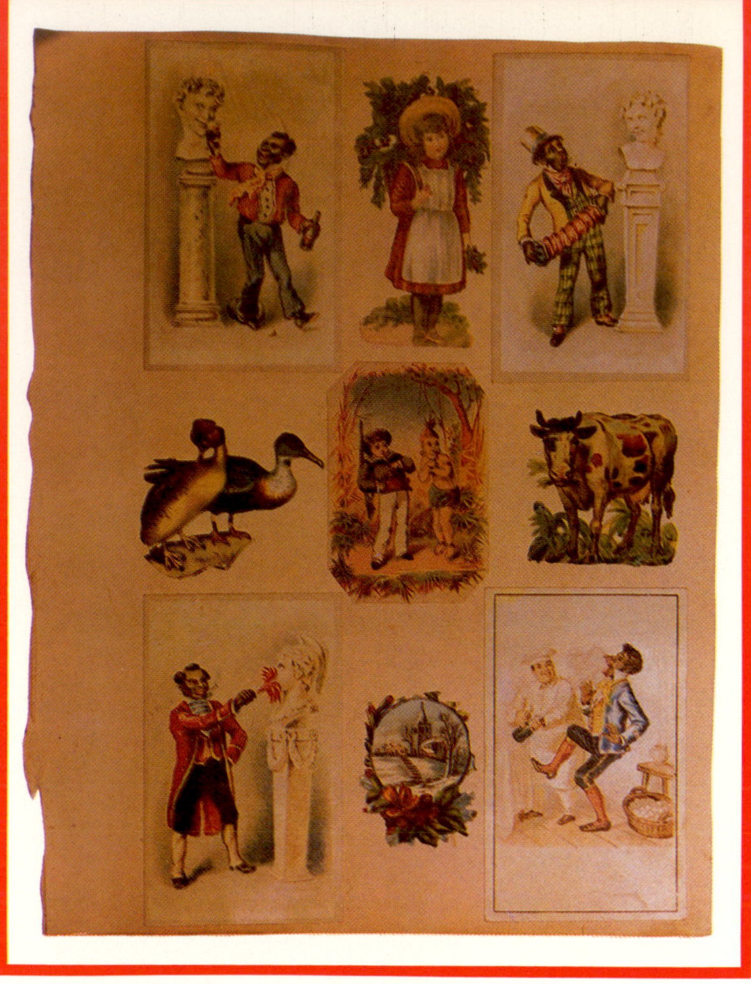

Typical page from a collection of trading and greeting cards, 1910. Courtesy of a private collection.

Comic cards. *Courtesy of Holt's Country Store, Grandview, Missouri.*

Set of die-cut minstrel figures, 7" tall. *Courtesy of Jim Morrison.*

Greeting card with moving features. German. *Courtesy of Holt's Country Store, Grandview, Missouri.*

Die-cut figure of a black dancer. Paper, 10". *Courtesy of Jim Morrison.*

Die-cut figures. *Courtesy of Jim Morrison.*

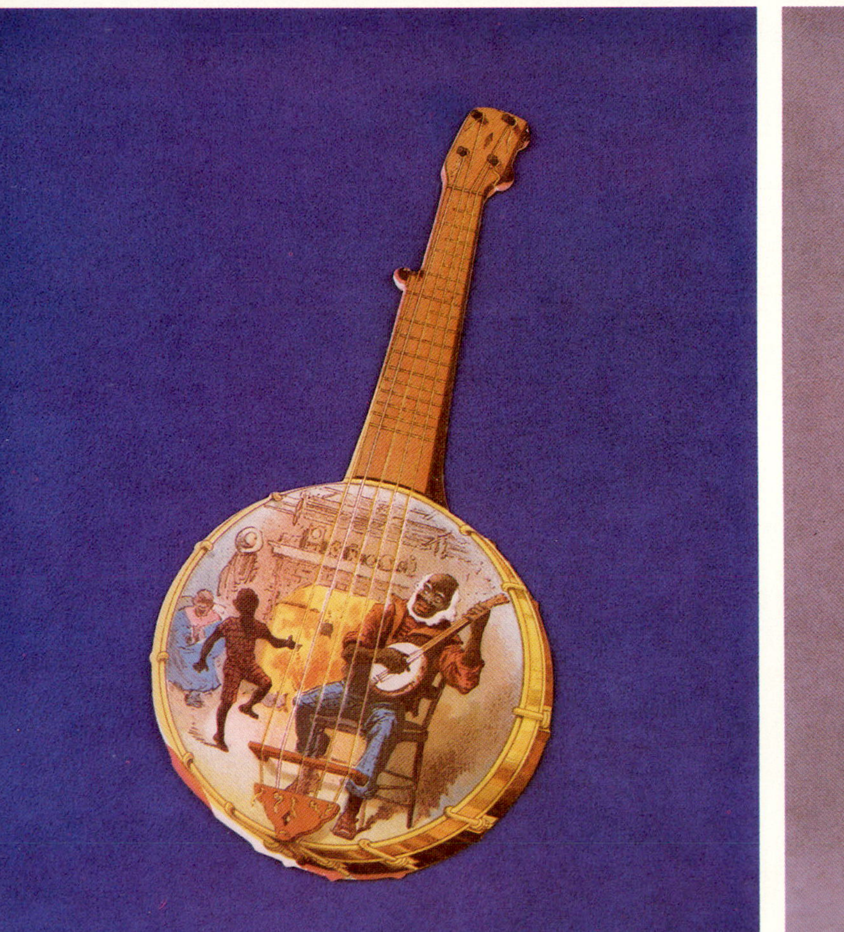

Die-cut banjo. *Courtesy of Jim Morrison.*

Die-cut 1929 calendar. *Courtesy of Jim Morrison.*

Stereoscope cards: top left, "Deed Child's, I's Didn't Know You's Was Dare," copyright 1898 by T.W. Ingersoll; top right "Did you say watermelon was no good?"; center left, "Blackberries and Milk," copyright 1894 by Strohmyer & Wyman, Publishers, New York; center right, sugar cane pickers; bottom, pickers grouped in cotton field, copyright 1892 by B.W. Kilburn. *Courtesy of a private collection.*

Periodicals

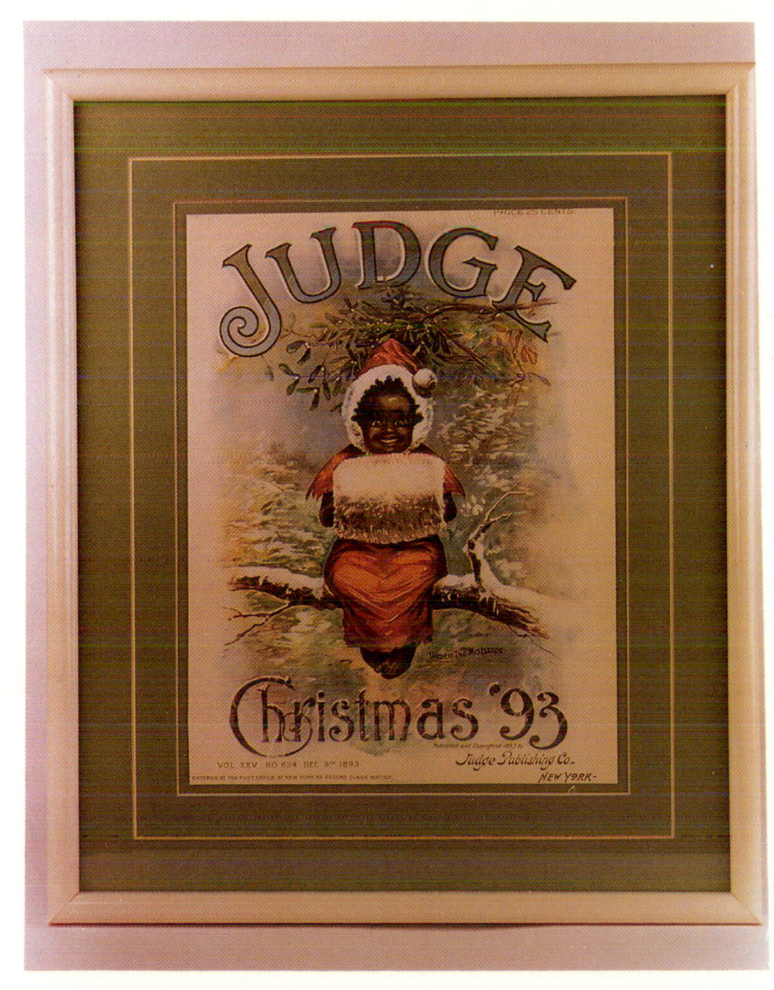

Judge, Christmas, 1893. Beginning in the 1880s this weekly publication offered political satire, commentary, and general entertainment. Its slant seemed to be toward the Republican Party while its rival magazine, *Punch*, favored the Democrats. Often *Judge* featured black figures on its cover and in its stories, though they usually reflected the stereotypes of the times. This cover illustration is entitled "Under the Mistletoe." Judge Publishing Co., New York. *Courtesy of Holt's Country Store, Grandview, Missouri.*

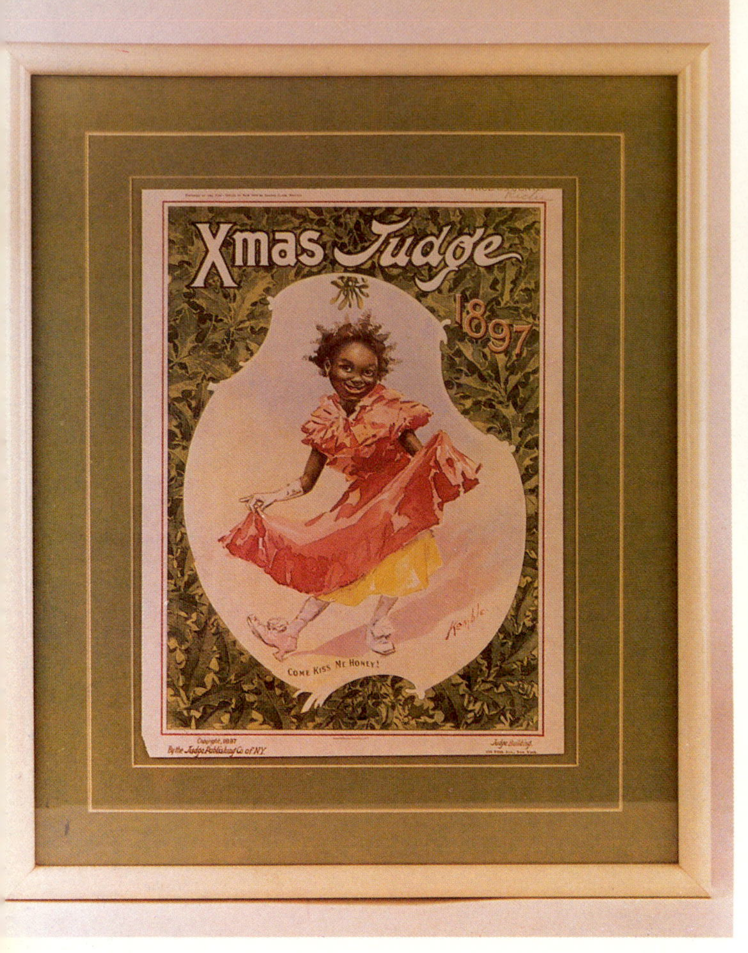

Cover of the *Christmas Judge*, December 18th, 1897. The print is entitled "Come Kiss Me Honey!" and is by Kemble. Copyright 1897 by the Judge Publishing Company of New York. *Courtesy of Holt's Country Store, Grandview, Missouri.*

Full-color lithograph in the *Christmas Judge*, 1897. Entitled "Made Greater by Contrast" it may have been drawn by Zimm. The humorous dialogue reads "Mammy Blackey (in surprise)—'Lan' saik, 'Cindy! w'y yo' hang up de baby's stockin' 'stid ob yo' own, foh youah C'rismus presunts?' Lucinda (disconsolately)—'Kase, mammy, de presunts i allus gits do look so pow'ful small w'en dey am in mah stockin'.'" *Courtesy of a private collection.*

Engraving illustrating a story in the *Christmas Judge*, 1897. Entitled "The Interrupted Christmas Dinner" it was drawn by P. Newell, New York. *Courtesy of a private collection.*

Engraving in the *Christmas Judge*, 1897. Entitled "He'd Rather Have the Old Kind" it was drawn by Kemble. The humorous dialogue reads "This is the latest thing in razors—the safety razor." "Dat may do, sah, fo' shavin'; but fo' a weddin' or social function it am puffictly useless." *Courtesy of a private collection.*

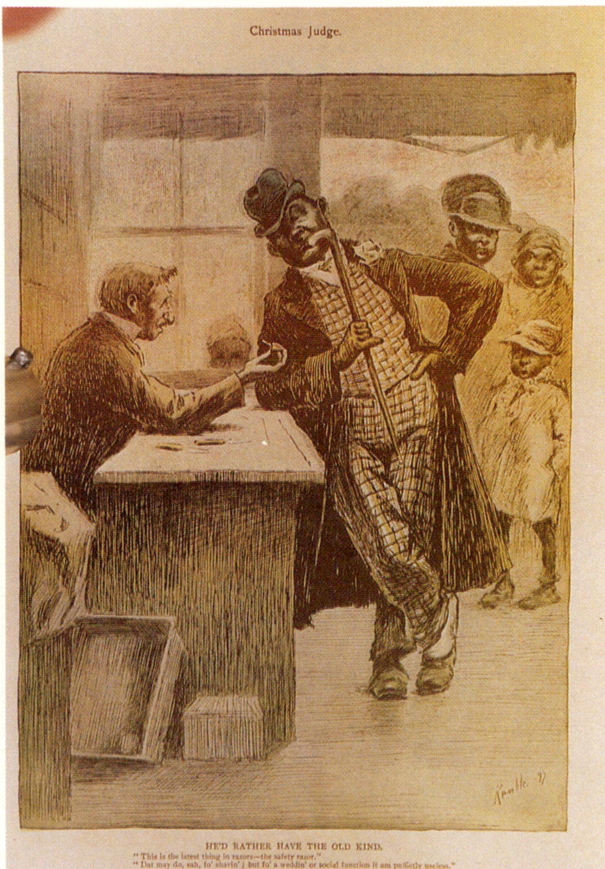

The "Pore Lil Mose" cartoons ran in the *New York Herald* at the turn of the century. Created by R. F. Outcault, they featured misadventures, philosophy, and ruminations of Pore Lil Mose in dialect and with full color illustrations featuring a highly stereotypical family and friends. Copyright the New York Herald Company, ca. 1901. *Courtesy of a private collection*.

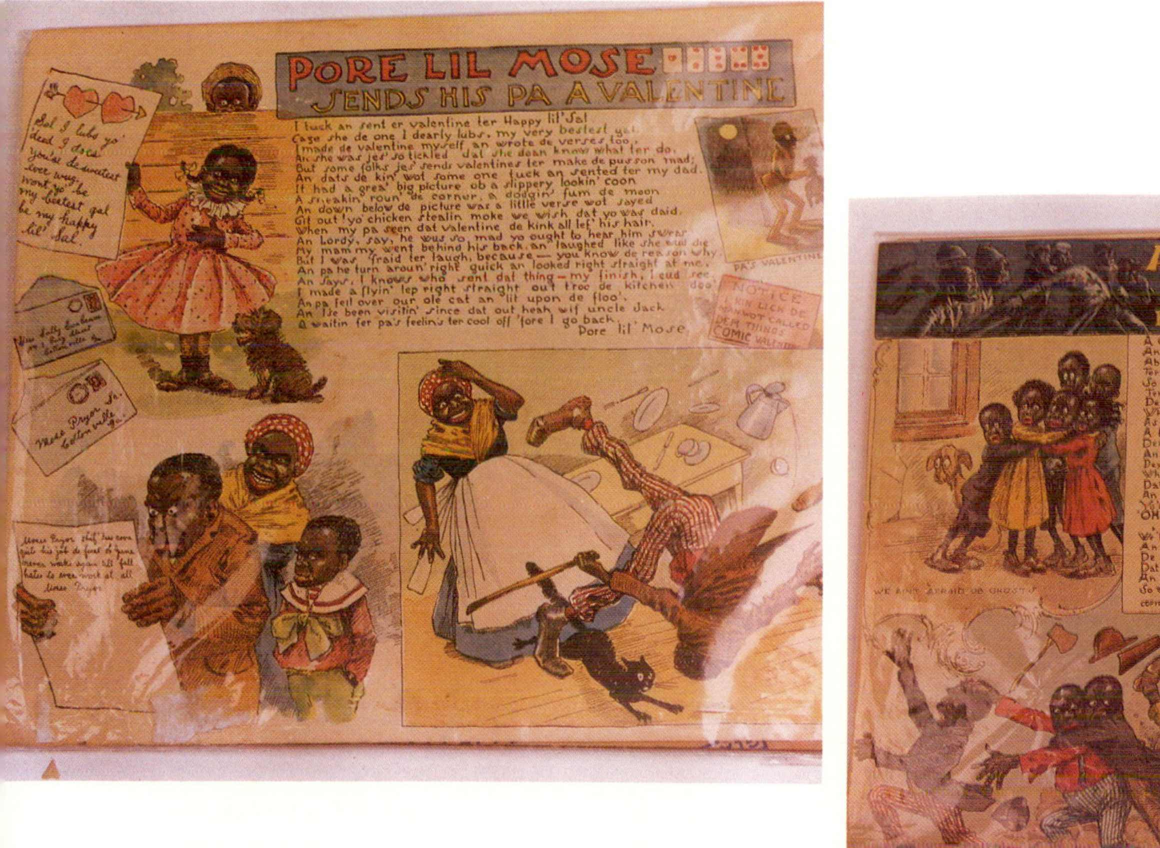

DE BURGLAR BRIGADE
AS TOLD BY
POOR LIL' MOSE
R.F. Outcault

Lil' Mose's Dog—Pore Lil' Dog
LIL' MOSE'S MOUSE HOUN'
R.F. Outcault

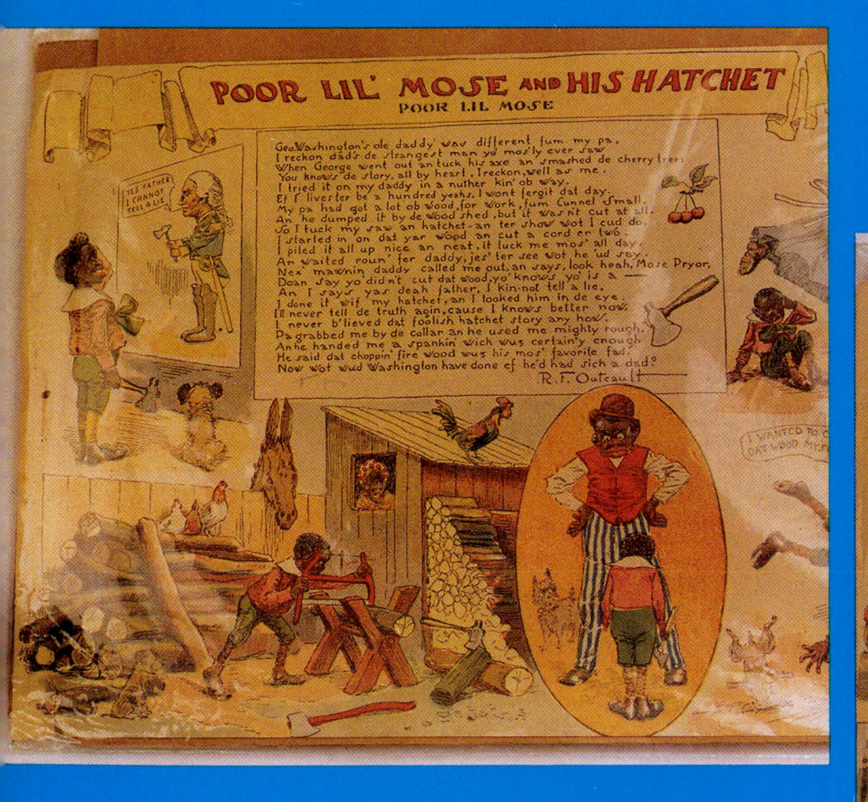

POOR LIL' MOSE AND HIS HATCHET
POOR LIL MOSE
Geo.Washington's ole daddy was different fum my pa,
I reckon dad's de strangest man yo' mos'ly ever saw
When George went out an tuck his axe an smashed de cherry tree:
You knows de story, all by heart, I reckon, well as me.
I tried it on my daddy in a nuther kin' ob way.
Ef I lives ter be a hundred yeahs, I wont fergit dat day.
My pa had got a lot ob wood, for work, fum Cunnel Small,
An he dumped it by de wood shed, but it was n't cut at all.
So I tuck my saw an hatchet - an ter show wot I cud do.
I started in on dat yar wood an cut a cord er two.
I piled it all up nice an neat, it tuck me mos' all day,
An waited roun' fer daddy, jes' ter see wot he 'ud say.
Nex' mawnin daddy called me out, an says, look heah, Mose Pryor,
Doan say yo' did n't cut dat wood, yo' knows yo' is a —
An I says yas deah father, I kin-not tell a lie,
I done it wif my hatchet, an I looked him in de eye.
I'll never tell de truth agin, cause I knows better now,
I never b'lieved dat foolish hatchet story any how.
Pa grabbed me by de collar an he used me mighty rough,
An he handed me a spankin' wich wus certain'y enough
He said dat choppin' fire wood wus his mos' favorite fad.
Now wot wud Washington have done ef he'd had sich a dad?
R.F. Outcault

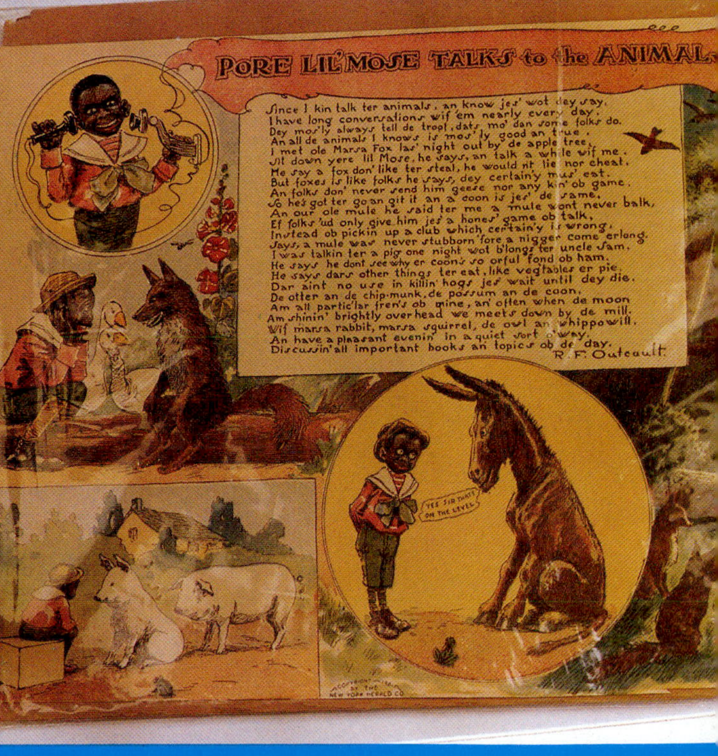

PORE LIL' MOSE TALKS to the ANIMALS
Since I kin talk ter animals, an know jes' wot dey say,
I have long conversations wif 'em nearly every day.
Dey mos'ly always tell de troot, dats mo' dan some folks do.
An all de animals I knows is mos'ly good an true.
I met ole Marsa Fox las' night out by de apple tree,
Sit down yere lil Mose, he says, an talk a while wif me.
He say a fox don' like ter steal, he would n't lie nor cheat.
But foxes is like folks he says, dey certain'y mus' eat.
An folks don' never send him geese nor any kin' ob game.
So he's got ter go an git it an a coon is jes' de same.
An our ole mule he said ter me a mule wont never balk,
Ef folks 'ud only give him jes' a hones' game ob talk,
Instead ob pickin up a club which certain'y is wrong.
Says, a mule was never stubborn 'fore a nigger come erlong.
I was talkin ter a pig one night wot b'longs ter uncle Sam.
He says he dont see why er coon's so orful fond ob ham.
He says dars other things ter eat, like vegtables er pie.
Dar aint no use in killin' hogs jes wait until dey die.
De otter an de chip-munk, de possum an de coon.
Am all partic'lar fren's ob mine, an' often when de moon
Am shinin' brightly overhead we meets down by de mill.
Wif marsa rabbit, marsa squirrel, de owl an whippowill.
An have a pleasant evenin' in a quiet sort o'way.
Discussin' all important books an topics ob de day.
R.F. Outcault

Part Three: For the Home

Flat Art

The image of African-Americans has long been a part of the American home. The elegance of some of the finer toys, or the beauty of lithographed advertisements and packaging of the late eighteenth century led to their being given a place of honor long after their original purpose was complete. Other items of flat art or figural pieces were created expressly for decoration. Still other objects were made to serve a functional purpose, from ashtrays to canisters. Like toys and advertising, these items relied largely on stereotypes for their design, although there are some notable exceptions.

Many of the figural pieces originated as souvenirs, prizes, or novelties. Images of blacks fishing, picking cotton, or eating watermelon are common forms. So are figures that rely on "potty humor" or sexual innuendo. It is certain that some of the images would have been unacceptable and unmarketable had the characters been white.

Domestics and servants, again, have enjoyed great popularity as household items. This is particularly true in the kitchen where cookie jars, salt and pepper shakers, canisters, towels, pot-holders, and a variety of other objects are designed in the images of Mammy, Uncle, or the chef. The Aunt Jemima Company offered many of these items to their customers as premiums in the 1940s and 1950s.

Flat art representations were also created for the home. Currier & Ives published a series of "Darktown" lithographs in the 1880s and 1890s that found widespread popularity. Other lithographs also made their way to the walls of American homes. Some were specifically created for the purpose and others, which had been designed for advertising, were framed and cherished for their artistic merit.

Portraiture and fine artistic representations of black people were exceedingly rare through the nineteenth century. The invention of photography brought the possibility of rendering an image of a black person that was true. Formal photographs of black men and women dating to the late 1800s are avidly sought after today, particularly by African-American collectors.

Included in Part III are some of the artifacts of the Jim Crow laws that governed much of the South from the 1870s through the 1950s. They are here by default, because they did not fit elsewhere. But perhaps they serve as a reminder. While images of African-Americans were finding their way into the homes of American whites, a large segment of the black population of America was kept out of schools, restaurants, restrooms, and the front seats of busses.

By looking at the evidence of material culture included in these pages, it is possible to trace history of the image of African-Americans. As we have seen, that material culture has rarely portrayed the African-American realistically. Instead it has relied on the half-truths of stereotype and exaggeration of popular culture for its images. When these popular misconceptions and stereotypes are given shape and form as toys, advertising, and a myriad of other objects, they give credibility to the images and carry them into the future.

"Two Nile-ists." Lithograph, unsigned. *Courtesy of Elizabeth Holt and Scott Lofquist.*

In the past thirty-five years much effort and commitment has gone into breaking free of this self-perpetuating circle. Society has come a long way, but the distance to travel is great and we still have a way to go. Perhaps this look at the past will, at the very least, help us to avoid repeating our mistakes.

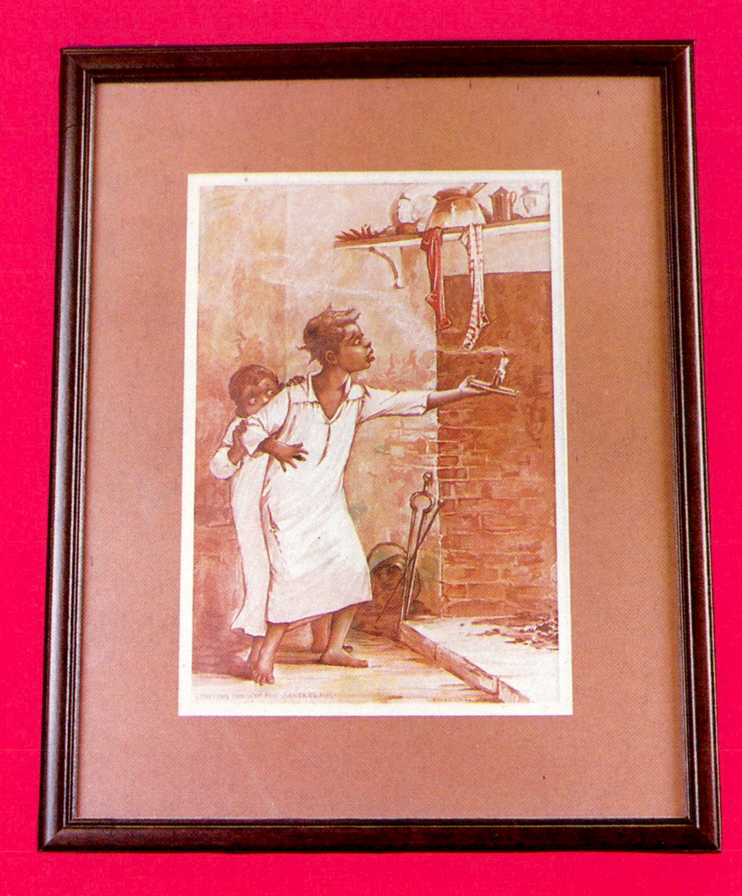

"Lighting the Way for Santa Claus," G.M. Auer & Co., Lith., New York. *Courtesy of Holt's Country Store, Grandview, Missouri.*

"The Darktown Fire Brigade—To The Rescue!" Lithograph on paper by Thomas Worth, copyright 1884 by Currier & Ives, New York.

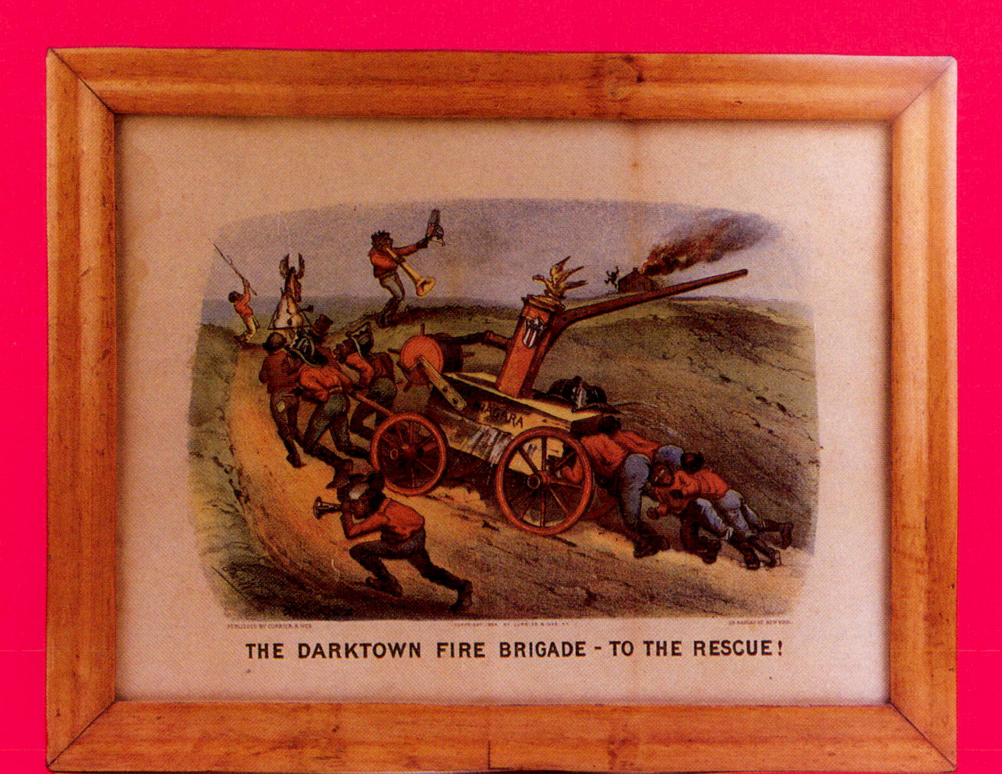
THE DARKTOWN FIRE BRIGADE - TO THE RESCUE!

"Comparing Notes." Lithograph copyright 1905 by the Welman Manufacturing Co. *Courtesy of Holt's Country Store, Grandview, Missouri.*

"A Huckleberry in a Bowl of Cream." Lithograph copyright 1915 by Morris & Bendien, New York. *Courtesy of a private collection.*

"Look Out for Blackmail!" C. Twelvetrees (?), ca. 1915. *Courtesy of a private collection.*

"Watch on the Rine." Lithograph signed Peyton. *Courtesy of Holt's Country Store, Grandview, Missouri.*

"A Nigger in the Woodpile." C. Twelvetrees (?), copyright 1916 by Morris & Bendien, New York. *Courtesy of a private collection.*

Two "penny dreadful" valentines, both lithographed caricatures and words of wisdom. Signed "H." and printed in the U.S. *Courtesy of Holt's Country Store, Grandview, Missouri.*

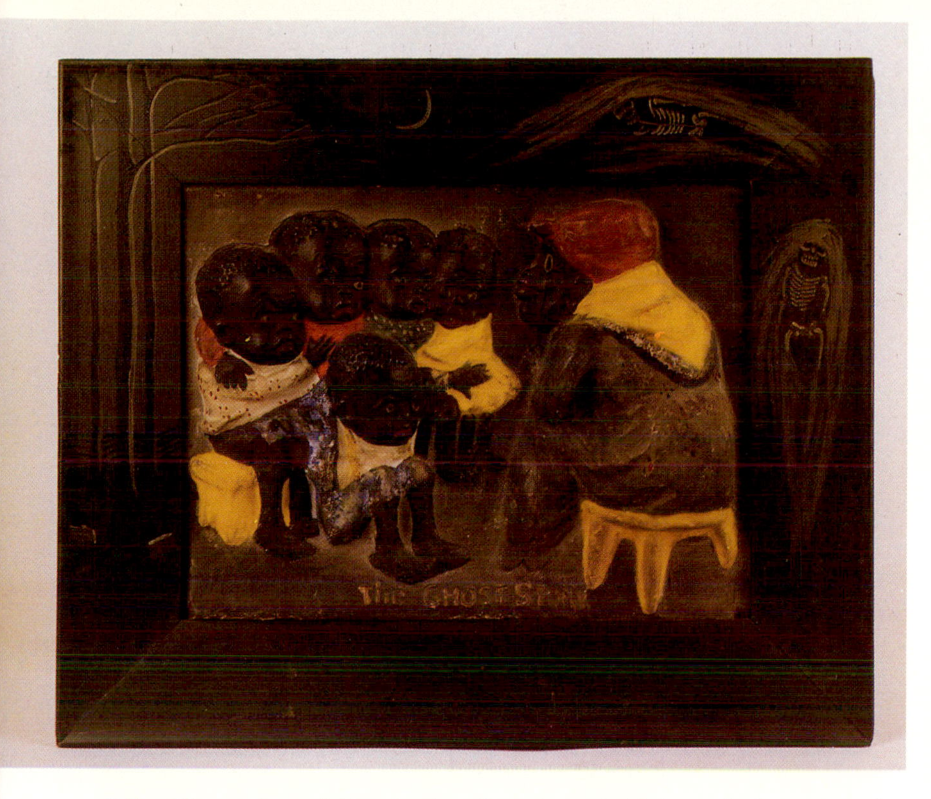

"The Ghost Story." Hand-painted papier mâché bas-relief in painted wood frame. *Courtesy of Holt's Country Store, Grandview, Missouri.*

Tinted photograph. *Courtesy of Holt's Country Store, Grandview, Missouri.*

Die-Cuts

Child and puppy die-cut paper figure. *Courtesy of Holt's Country Store, Grandview, Missouri.*

"I'se used to whippin'. Golly! I'se so wicked." Die-cut lithographed paper figure. *Courtesy of Holt's Country Store, Grandview, Missouri.*

Four unhappy black children in a basket. Die-cut lithographed paper figure. *Courtesy of Holt's Country Store, Grandview, Missouri.*

Large Christmas ornament. Die-cut figure, paper, fabric and cotton. *Courtesy of Jim Large*

Other

Oil on chestnut painting of a woman in the Creole-manner, signed Simon Mans (?). 10.25" x 7.75", ca. 1890. *Courtesy of Milton E. Schedivy.*

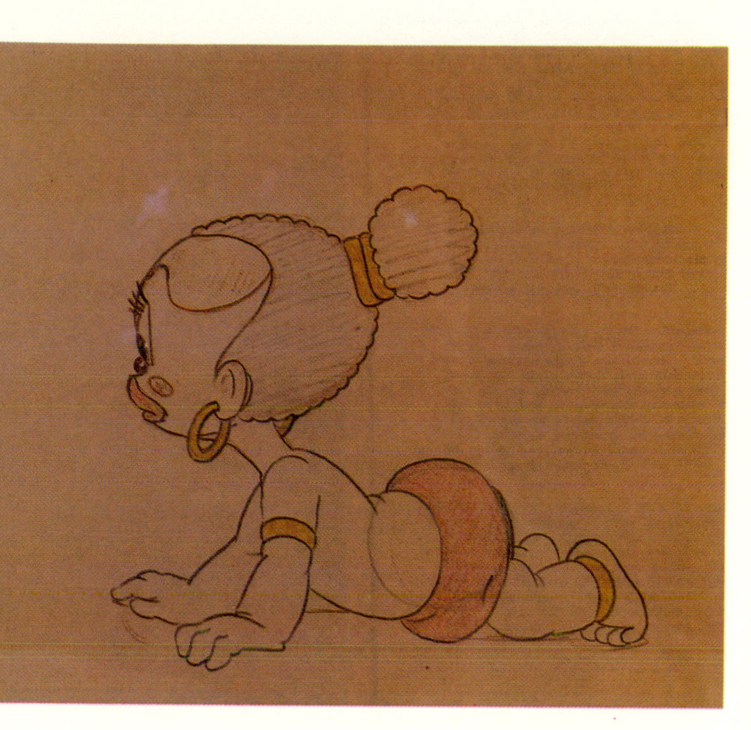

Drawing from "Inky and the Lion." Chuck Jones, 1941. *Courtesy of Gifted Images.*

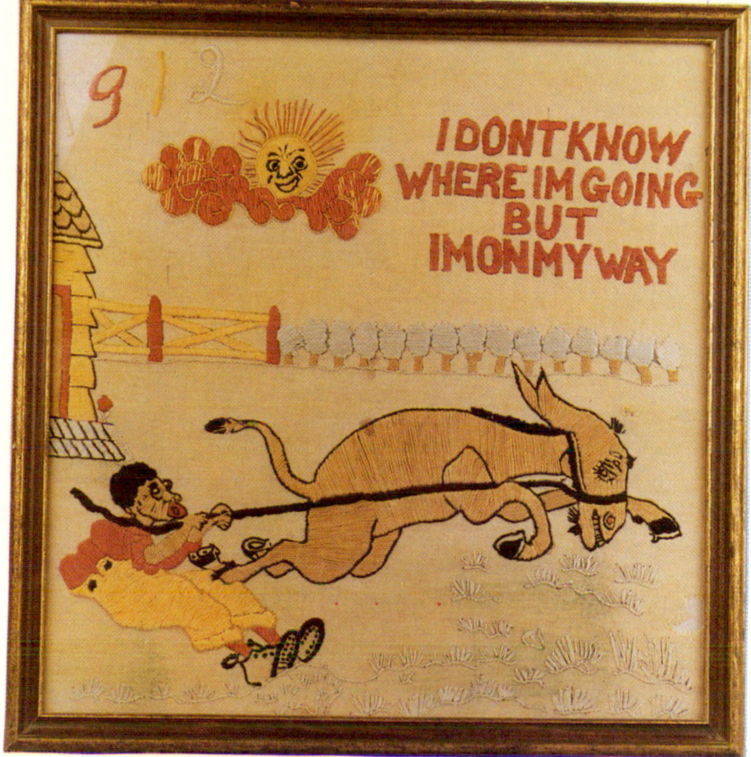

"I don't know where I'm going but I'm on my way." Needlework art, 1912. *Courtesy of Holt's Country Store, Grandview, Missouri.*

Negro League baseball tickets. Top: 1947 World Series; bottom, 1948 All-Star game. *Courtesy of Don Flanagan.*

Sign from the Lonestar Restaurant Association, Dallas, Texas, and supplied to its members. Front and back shown. *Courtesy of Holt's Country Store, Grandview, Missouri.*

Restaurant sign. Marked "A.A. Signs, May 5, 1931." *Courtesy of Elizabeth Holt and Scott Lofquist.*

Sign for a black theater. Marked "Knox Theater—Augusta, GA." Manufactured by the Ace Sign Co. *Courtesy of Holt's Country Store, Grandview, Missouri.*

Metal rental sign. *Courtesy of Holt's Country Store, Grandview, Missouri.*

Figures

Fishing

Figure fishing. Chalkware, 4". *Courtesy of Holt's Country Store, Grandview, Missouri.*

Chalkware fishing figure, polychrome finish. *Courtesy of Holt's Country Store, Grandview, Missouri.*

Cotton

Mammy figure of pipe cleaner and fabric with broom on cotton bale. *Courtesy of Holt's Country Store, Grandview, Missouri.*

Plastic figures on cotton bales. The bale on the right is marked, "I am from Dixie, Miniature Cotton Bale, Souvenir." *Courtesy of Holt's Country Store, Grandview, Missouri.*

Figure eating watermelon on bale of cotton. 1.5" x 1". *Courtesy of Holt's Country Store, Grandview, Missouri.*

Left: A souvenir of Memphis, Tennessee, the watermelon eating figure is seated on a pin cushion under of tree of cotton. The design for this piece was patented by Joseph Hollander of Baton Rouge, Louisiana in 1938. Right: plastic figure on bale of cotton eating watermelon. *Courtesy of Holt's Country Store, Grandview, Missouri.*

Bisque figure of a black man standing beside cotton bails. Polychrome finish. *Courtesy of a private collection.*

Plastic sharecroppers with bags of cotton. *Courtesy of Charlene Upham.*

Watermelon

Ceramic ashtray in the shape of a child eating watermelon. Marked "A Souvenir of the Shenandoah Valley, VA.," circa 1920. *Courtesy of Frank G. Whitson, Baltimore, Maryland.*

Ceramic "Mopsy" figure 3.5" high. *Courtesy of Jagg Antiques.*

Three ceramic figures. *Courtesy of Holt's Country Store, Grandview, Missouri.*

Four chalkware figures. *Courtesy of Holt's Country Store, Grandview, Missouri.*

A wooden sculpture by Charles Spiron of North Carolina, 1990. *Courtesy of Seacrest Antiques.*

Tin bucket signed "Converse" with lithographed image of a black person eating watermelon. *Courtesy of Holt's Country Store, Grandview, Missouri.*

Figure on a chamber pot holding watermelon. *Courtesy of Holt's Country Store, Grandview, Missouri.*

Potty Humor

The pain is obvious in this metal incense burner. National Products Inc., Chicago, Illinois. 6″ tall, 1920s—1930s. *Courtesy of Jan Lindenberger, Black By Popular Demand, Colorado Springs, Colorado.*

Four outhouse figures in bisque. Many of these were imported from Japan in the late-1940s and 1950s. *Courtesy of Holt's Country Store, Grandview, Missouri.*

Typical bisque outhouse figure, of the type usually sold as souvenirs. 2.5″ tall. *Courtesy of Bunny Walker.*

"Diaper Dan—Weather Forecaster and Thermometer." His diaper is treated to turn blue when the humidity is low and pink when it is high. Multi Products Inc., Chicago, copyright 1949. 5″ high x 4″ wide. *Courtesy of Jan Lindenberger, Black By Popular Demand, Colorado Springs, Colorado.*

Sexual Humor

"The Voyeur" has a black man peering through the curtains at a white woman in her bath. While seemingly a simple humorous image, it must be seen in light of the fear that white women were sexual "targets" of black men, and the numerous lynchings this fear engendered. Bisque. *Courtesy of Holt's Country Store, Grandview, Missouri.*

"Before and After." Bisque three piece novelty piece. *Courtesy of Holt's Country Store, Grandview, Missouri.*

This piece and the next present a recurring theme in novelty pieces. This is a tourist novelty marked "Gap," and was probably manufactured in Japan. 3″ high. *Courtesy of Holt's Country Store, Grandview, Missouri.*

Roughly sculpted salt rock, 3″ high. *Courtesy of Jan Lindenberger, Black By Popular Demand, Colorado Springs, Colorado.*

For whatever reason this ashtray was a successful item, selling principally as a souvenir. It was made in several variations, three of which are shown here. *Courtesy of Jan Lindenberger, Black By Popular Demand, Colorado Springs, Colorado.*

The fascination with breasts continues in these swizzle sticks purporting to show the process of aging. Entitled "Zulu Lulus," they are 6" high. *Courtesy of Howard and Myra Whitelaw.*

Seated couples manufactured in pot metal. *Courtesy of Atlantiques.*

Domestics and Servers

Except for the cook at the far right, these pottery pieces are designed as wall hangings, and could be used as planters or holders for other items. The cook is a spoon holder. 5.5"-6". *Courtesy of Jan Lindenberger, Black By Popular Demand, Colorado Springs, Colorado.*

This roly-poly butler, roughly shaped of a composition material. *Courtesy of a private collection.*

Chef figure, composition material and linen. *Courtesy of a private collection.*

This cut-out wooden mammy is hand-painted and stands 30 inches high. The figure was a lawn decoration designed to hold the water hose. She probably once had a pipe in her mouth. *Courtesy of Jan Lindenberger, Black By Popular Demand, Colorado Springs, Colorado.*

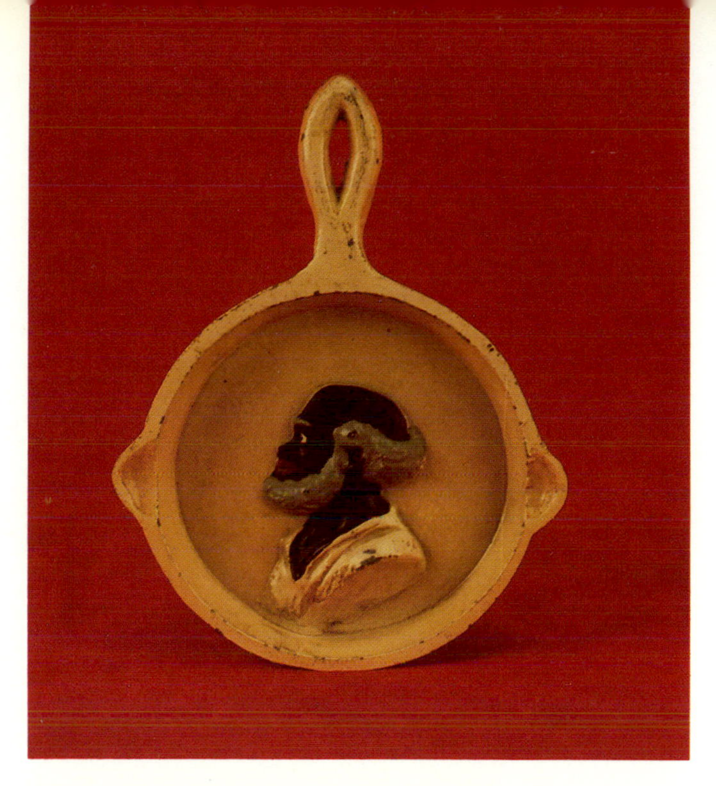

Cast iron wall hanging. 6″ tall. *Courtesy of Jan Lindenberger, Black By Popular Demand, Colorado Springs, Colorado.*

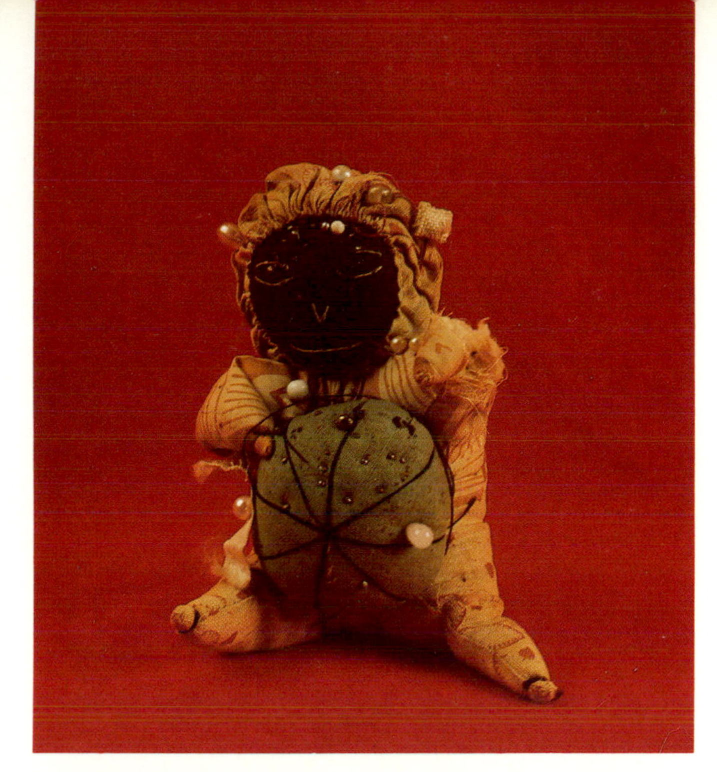

Pin cushion, 4.5″ high. *Courtesy of Jan Lindenberger, Black By Popular Demand, Colorado Springs, Colorado.*

Cast iron andirons in the mammy design. 15.5″ high x 9.5″ wide x 15.5″ deep. *Courtesy of House of Stuart, Centerport, New York.*

A rare cast iron soap dish. 5″ high. *Courtesy of Jan Lindenberger, Black By Popular Demand, Colorado Springs, Colorado.*

Souvenir mammy pin cushion, marked Eldorado Springs, Missouri. Of wood and fabric, 5.5″ high. *Courtesy of Jan Lindenberger, Black By Popular Demand, Colorado Springs, Colorado.*

Very rare cast iron, hand-painted paper weight, ca. 1910. 4.25″ tall. *Courtesy of Pat and Rich Garthoeffner.*

Ceramic string dispenser, marked N.S. Company, U.S.A. *Courtesy of Jan Lindenberger, Black By Popular Demand, Colorado Springs, Colorado.*

Porcelain wall sconce, with metal and plastic electrical fixture. 7″ tall. *Courtesy of Jan Lindenberger, Black By Popular Demand, Colorado Springs, Colorado.*

Table lamp. *Courtesy of Atlantiques.*

Primitive bisque mammy figure. *Courtesy of a private collection.*

Doorstop of porcelain on cast iron, the Chicago Vitreous Enamel Products Company, Chicago, Illinois. 7″ tall. *Courtesy of Frank G. Whitson, Baltimore, Maryland.*

Bisque planter in the form of field hand. 18″ x 10″. *Courtesy of Holt's Country Store, Grandview, Missouri.*

Ceramic ashtray holder originally came with four ashtrays and a lid, made in Japan. *Courtesy of Jan Lindenberger, Black By Popular Demand, Colorado Springs, Colorado.*

Ceramic mammy planter. *Courtesy of Jan Lindenberger, Black By Popular Demand, Colorado Springs, Colorado.*

Metal basket with figures. *Courtesy of Holt's Country Store, Grandview, Missouri.*

If complete this Maruron Ware ceramic cracker jar would have a wicker handle and a flowered hat, made in Japan. *Courtesy of Jan Lindenberger, Black By Popular Demand, Colorado Springs, Colorado.*

Other Figures

Majolica humidor made in Germany, in the 1920s. The top of its hat is missing. If complete it would be 7" tall. *Courtesy of Jan Lindenberger, Black By Popular Demand, Colorado Springs, Colorado.*

The head from a "Dancing Darky" cigar store figure. This is similar to a figure from the N.Y. Historical Society dated to the mid-nineteenth century. Polychrome on pine. 9" high (The complete figure measured approximately 52" high. *Courtesy of Frank G. Whitson, Baltimore, Maryland.*

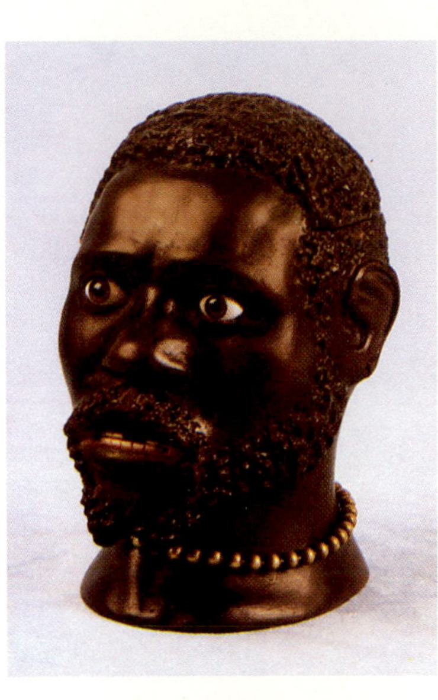

Carved ebony cigarette box with paperweight glass eyes and ivory teeth. Late 1800s. *Courtesy of Allan Kessler, Chicago.*

Carved ebony inkwell with paperweight glass eyes and a porcelain insert. 5″ tall. *Courtesy of Allan Kessler, Chicago.*

Full-sized cast iron cigar store figure, cigars missing. Cast in 1950 by the Hamilton Foundry and Machine Co., Hamilton, Ohio. One of three cast. The use of black figures for cigar stores probably began in England, where some confusion between Indians and blacks seemed to exist, creating Indians with black features. Cigar stores in New York, searching for new symbols, began to use black people in common, though stereotypical, appearance and dress. This nicely sculpted piece is 38″ tall seated. *Courtesy of Clifton Anderson.*

Ceramic tobacco pipe. *Courtesy of a private collection.*

Clay pipe, 7" long. Pre-1930. *Courtesy of Frank G. Whitson, Baltimore, Maryland.*

Carved briar pipe, with polychrome finish. 6" long. *Courtesy of Frank G. Whitson, Baltimore, Maryland.*

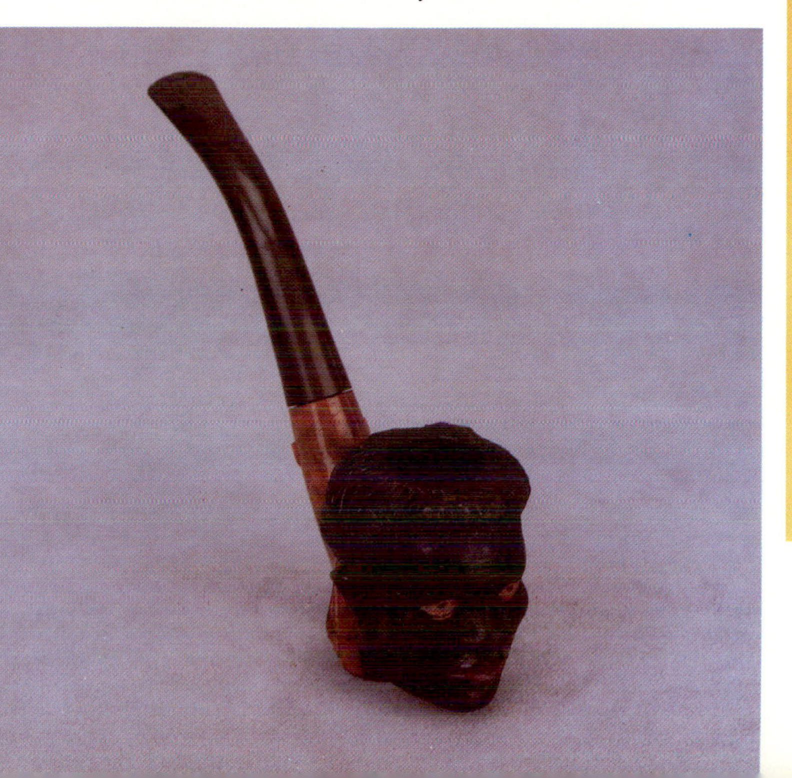

Clay figural pipe. 3" high x 6" long. *Courtesy of Jan Lindenberger, Black By Popular Demand, Colorado Springs, Colorado.*

Cut-out wooden ashtray figure. *Courtesy of Fran and Jim Pohrer.*

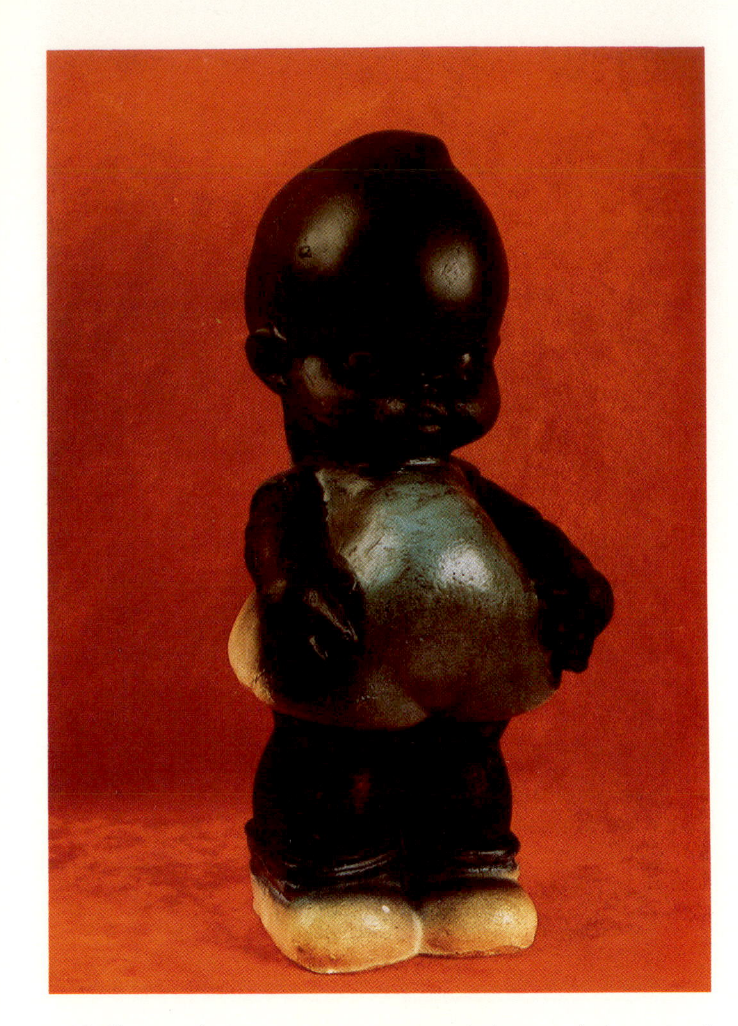

Chalkware figure. *Courtesy of Jan Lindenberger, Black By Popular Demand, Colorado Springs, Colorado.*

"Snow Flake" ceramic baby. *Courtesy of Holt's Country Store, Grandview, Missouri.*

Two ceramic figures. The right figure has a bobbing head. *Courtesy of a private collection.*

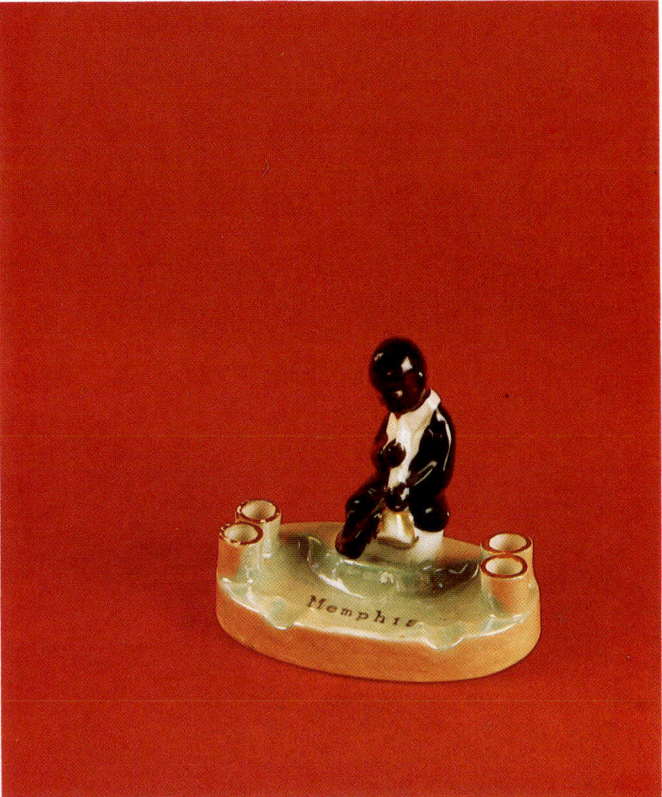

Ceramic cigarette holder and ashtray. Japan. *Courtesy of Jan Lindenberger, Black By Popular Demand, Colorado Springs, Colorado.*

Two souvenir dandies. Both carry roses, and the one on the right is marked: "Cedar Point, Ohio." *Courtesy of Jan Lindenberger, Black By Popular Demand, Colorado Springs, Colorado.*

Four celluloid figures in red. *Courtesy of Holt's Country Store, Grandview, Missouri.*

Plastic doll-rattle. *Courtesy of Jan Lindenberger, Black By Popular Demand, Colorado Springs, Colorado.*

Baby doll. *Courtesy of a private collection.*

Ceramic Kewpee doll. *Courtesy of Holt's Country Store, Grandview, Missouri.*

Two celluloid figures. *Courtesy of Holt's Country Store, Grandview, Missouri.*

Ceramic craps shooters with die. *Courtesy of Jan Lindenberger, Black By Popular Demand, Colorado Springs, Colorado.*

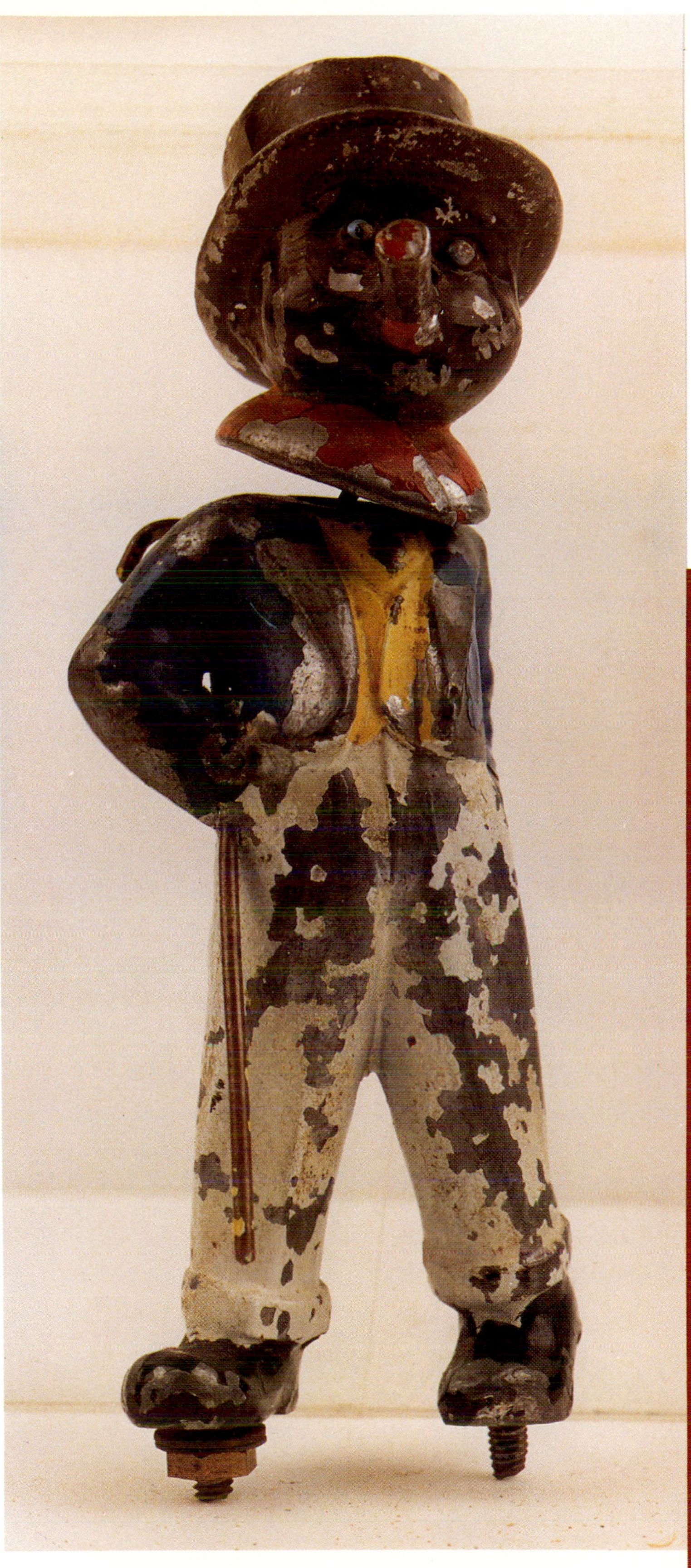

Metal figure. 4.5″ tall. *Courtesy of a private collection.*

Jointed complete bellows minstrel figure, constructed of wood, papier mâché, wire and fabric. Squeak toy—press tummy and he tips his hat. *Courtesy of a private collection.*

Ceramic Louis "Satchmo" Armstrong planter, possibly still in production. *Courtesy of Ladybug's Cupboard.*

The jazz band is celluloid, with each figure being 2.5" tall. *Courtesy of Neat Olde Things, Stewartsville, New Jersey.*

Ceramic musicians on the couch. *Courtesy of Holt's Country Store, Grandview, Missouri.*

Though it looks as though someone took a hot iron and creased the head of this plastic figure, it is apparently part of the design. Perhaps this feature is necessary for the figure to make the whistling sound it promises, but it makes for one of the more distorted and grotesque representations encountered. "Georgie the Whistling Boy" was manufactured by the Irving Corporation of Fitchburg, Massachusetts. The tag reads "Wind me up and hear me whistle." *Courtesy of Gary Moss, Brookline, Massachusetts.*

Bobbing head folk figure. 5.5" tall. *Courtesy of Jan Lindenberger, Black By Popular Demand, Colorado Springs, Colorado.*

Wax spool with ceramic figure, used for waxing thread. *Courtesy of a private collection.*

Ashtray, probably German, ca. 1910. 4.5″ tall. *Neat Olde Things, Stewartsville, New Jersey.*

Sleeping child figure. Approximately 12″ long, and constructed of painted plaster, ca. 1950. *Courtesy of Clifton Anderson.*

Two Vargas figures. New Orleans. *Courtesy of Charlene Upham.*

Household Items

Cookie Jars

Plastic cookie jar given as a premium by Aunt Jemima, early 1950s. 10.5" tall. *Courtesy of Jan Lindenberger, Black By Popular Demand, Colorado Springs, Colorado.*

Plastic cookie jar manufactured by F & F Plastic Co., for Aunt Jemima, ca. 1948. 12" tall. *Courtesy of Jan Lindenberger, Black By Popular Demand, Colorado Springs, Colorado.*

McCoy ceramic cookie jar, ca. 1940s. 11″ tall. *Courtesy of Jan Lindenberger, Black By Popular Demand, Colorado Springs, Colorado.*

Ceramic cookie jar manufactured by National Silver Company, New York in the 1940s. 10″ tall. *Courtesy of Jan Lindenberger, Black By Popular Demand, Colorado Springs, Colorado.*

Contemporary ceramic cookie jar. 12″ tall. *Courtesy of Jan Lindenberger, Black By Popular Demand, Colorado Springs, Colorado.*

Yellow ceramic cookie jar with 22k gold trim. Pearl China Company, U.S.A. 7.5″ tall. *Courtesy of Jan Lindenberger, Black By Popular Demand, Colorado Springs, Colorado.*

Ceramic cookie jar distributed by the National Silver Company of New York, early 1940s. 9″ tall. *Courtesy of Jan Lindenberger, Black By Popular Demand, Colorado Springs, Colorado.*

Brown ceramic cookie jar, early 1960s. *Courtesy of Jan Lindenberger, Black By Popular Demand, Colorado Springs, Colorado.*

Contemporary cookie jar with raised mammy figure. Ceramic, 14″ tall. *Courtesy of Jan Lindenberger, Black By Popular Demand, Colorado Springs, Colorado.*

A contemporary cookie jar by Rick Wisecarver. *Courtesy of Jan Lindenberger, Black By Popular Demand, Colorado Springs, Colorado.*

Other Containers

Bisque containers, 5″ tall. *Courtesy of Margaret B. Schiffer.*

Contemporary four piece canister set, 8″-12″. *Courtesy of Jan Lindenberger, Black By Popular Demand, Colorado Springs, Colorado.*

Aunt Jemima spice jars and rack. The plastic set was offered as a premium in the 1950s. F & F Mold and Die Company, Dayton, Ohio. Figures 4″ tall, stand 7″ tall. *Courtesy of Jan Lindenberger, Black By Popular Demand, Colorado Springs, Colorado.*

Oil and vinegar cruets with stoppers, ceramic and cork. Made in Japan, 5.5″ high. *Courtesy of Jan Lindenberger, Black By Popular Demand, Colorado Springs, Colorado.*

Salt and Pepper

Salt and pepper shakers customized as "Dick" and "Marguerite." *Courtesy of Jan Lindenberger, Black By Popular Demand, Colorado Springs, Colorado.*

Chef head salt and pepper by Anne Matheson. 5″ high. *Courtesy of Jan Lindenberger, Black By Popular Demand, Colorado Springs, Colorado.*

Ceramic salt and pepper shakers with tray, made in Japan. *Courtesy of Jan Lindenberger, Black By Popular Demand, Colorado Springs, Colorado.*

Ceramic porter with salt and pepper shakers as the bags he is carrying. Manufactured by Hinode of Japan. *Courtesy of Jan Lindenberger, Black By Popular Demand, Colorado Springs, Colorado.*

Four inch high ceramic salt and pepper shakers. *Courtesy of Jan Lindenberger, Black By Popular Demand, Colorado Springs, Colorado.*

Page	Position	Value
	TR	N/A
	B	175-225
63	T	125-140
	BL	85-125
	BR	30-40
64	T	325-380
	BL	380-450
	BR	350-400
65	T	100-125
	TR	350-400
	BR	350-400
66		Set 8000-10000
67	T	Each 35-45
	B	45-55
68	TL	Each 35-45
	TR	Each 35-45
	BL	Each 35-45
	BR	Tradecards 35-45
		Postcards 20-30
69	T	35-45
	BL	150-175
	BR	In good condition
		125-150
70	TL	65-75
	TR	275-300
	BL	35-40
	BC	60-70
	BR	Each 125-135
71	TL	195-225
	TR	375-400
	BL	125-135
	BC	350-375
	BR	200-225
72	TL	225-250
	TR	45-55
	BL	85-100
	BR	385-450
73	TL	N/A
	TR	60-70
	BL	275-300
	BR	25-35
74	T	N/A
	B	l: 325-350
		r: 240-265
75	TL	250-275
	TR	N/A
	BL	350-400
	BR	N/A
76		N/A
77	TL	N/A
	TR	125-150
	BL	N/A
	BR	125-150
78	TL	225-250
	TR	100-115
	B	l-r: 25, 35, 35, 60, 45, 45
79	TL	65-75
	TR	l: 25-30; r: 30-40
	BL	250-275
	BR	125-150
80	TL	55-60
	TR	55-70
	BL	l: 250-275; r: 35-45
	BR	300-350
81	T	60-70
	BL	125-150
	BR	45-55
82	TL	60-75
	TR	40-50
	BL	45-55
	BR	85-95
83	TL	35-45
	TR	45-55
	BL	30-40
	BR	40-50
84	TL	45-55

Page	Position	Value
	TR	35-35
	BL	65-75
85	TL	45-55
	TR	45-55
	BR	40-50
86	TL	50-60
	TR	60-70
	BL	75-85
87	TL	35-45
	TR	35-45
	BR	110-125
88	T	185-210
	B	N/A
89	T	N/A
	BL	35-45
	BR	15-20
90	T	Figures each 18-25
	B	125-150
91	TL	240-275
	TR	N/A
	BL	N/A
	BR	l: 125; r: 165
92	L	65-75
	TR	15-20
	BR	15-20
93	T	l-r: 185, 325, 275
	BL	45-55
	BR	60-75
94	TL	22-25
	TR	18-25
	BR	22-25
95	TL	45-50
	TR	15-20
	BL	25-30
	BR	Each 22-25
96	T	Each 25-30
	B	Top: 25-30; bottom: 12-18
97	T	25-30
	BL	18-22
	BR	12-15
98	TL	45-55
	TR	15-35
	B	Each 20-25
99	TL	Each 30-35
	BL	18-22
	BR	30-35
100	T	Each 22-25
	BL	35-40
	BR	40-45
101	T	Each 20-25
	B	35-40
102	TL	35-40
103		Each 45-60
104		Each 45-60
105	BR	N/A
106	T	N/A
	B	385-425
107	TR	65-75
	BL	35-45
	BR	N/A
108	T	125-150
	CR	N/A
	B	Each 45-50
109	TL	8000-10000
	TR	65-85
	BL	385-400
	BR	65-85
110	TL	65-85
	TR	125-150
	B	2500-3000
111	TL	N/A
	TR	45-50
	B	All Star: 300-500
		World Series: 350-600
112	T	165-185
	B	250-275

Page	Position	Value
113	T	250-275
	B	175-225
114	TL	45-55
	TR	125-140
	BR	25-35
115	TR	l: 60-70; r: 35-40
	LC	40-50
	BR	Each 25-35
116	T	125-140
	B	pair 125-150
117	T	45-55
	B	85-100
118	T	l-r: 65-85, 65-85, 45-55
	B	l-r: 60-70, 65-75, 45-55, 35-45
119	L	N/A
	TR	245-270
	BR	45-55
120	TL	125-150
	TR	15-35
	BL	Each 15-35
	BR	35-45
121	T	65-75
	B	45-55
122	TL	35-45
	TR	35-45
	B	45-60
123	TL	25-35
	TR	Each pair 185-225
	B	45-70
124	TL	N/A
	TR	185-210
	BL	125-150
125	TL	65-75
	TR	45-60
	B	Pair 285-325
126	TL	225-250
	TR	35-45
	BL	Rare
	BR	125-150
127	TL	325-360
	TR	N/A
	BL	135-150
	BR	N/A
128	TL	N/A
	TR	245-260
	BL	85-100
	BR	N/A
129	TL	If complete $760-800
	BL	As is $245, with hat 475
	R	Rare
130	L	N/A
	TR	475-525
	BR	600-625
131	TL	125-160
	TR	125-160
	CL	125-160
	BL	125-160
	BR	175-225
132	TL	125-150
	TR	45-60
	BL	l: 22-25 (as is); r: 65-75
	BR	45-55
133	TL	85-125
	TR	l-r: 65, 65, 65, 45
	BL	85-100
	BR	45-55
134	TL	185-200
	TR	l: 145, r: N/A
	B	Set 125-145
135	L	N/A
	R	N/A
136	T	65-75
	B	225-230
137	TL	85-100
	BL	275-300

Page	Position	Value
	R	25-35
138	TL	225-275
	TR	45-50
	B	Rare
139	T	Each 260-285
	BL	225-250
	BR	350-400
140	TL	185-200
	TR	265-280
	BL	30-60
	BR	400-425
141	TL	265-280
	TR	245-260
	BL	45-60
	BR	250-285
142	T	each 185
	B	285-300
143	TL	Each 35-40
	TR	Set 95-110
	BL	Set 45-55
	BR	Set 60-70
144	L	45-55
	TR	Set 40-50
	BR	Set 40-50
145	T	Set 45-60
	BL	Set 35-45
	BR	Set 60-70
146	T	Set 35-45
	B	125-135
147	TL	165-180
	BL	65-75
	R	65-80
148	TL	l: 110-125; r: 85-95
	TR	85-100
	BL	100-125
	BR	165-180
149	TL	65-80
	BL	Set 65
	R	22-25
150	TL	Pair 60-70
	TR	Set 45-60
	BL	45-60
151	L	35-40
	TR	40-50
	BR	65-75
152	TL	25-35
	TR	150-175
	BL	150-175
	BR	125-135
153	T	Set 350-375
	BL	145-200
	BR	N/A
154	TL	145-160
	TR	35-50
	CL	25-30
	B	40-50
155	L	N/A
	TR	l: 65-75; r: 10-25
	CR	l:35-40; r: 65-75
	BR	35-45
156	T	Rare
	BL	175-200
	BR	125-150
157	T	45-55
	B	Each 300-350
158	TL	365-400
	TR	350-325
	BL	300-325
	BR	N/A
159	TR	6500-8000
	BL	N/A
	BR	N/A
160	L	1500-3000

IMAGES IN BLACK

150 Years of Black Collectibles

VALUE GUIDE

Values vary immensely according to the condition of the piece, the location of the market, and the overall quality of the design and manufacture. While one must make their own decisions, we can offer a guide. The prices given are estimates of pieces in excellent condition, unless otherwise noted.

Two cautions for the collector. First, since black collectibles cross different collecting fields, a value guide sometimes is greatly out of line. We have tried to catch these aberrations where possible, but some may have slipped by us. An example is the baseball tickets on page 111. In our first draft we priced them at $35-50 apiece, a price from a collector of black memorabilia. Upon checking with a sports memorabilia collector, however, we found their value to be more in the range of $300-600. So be careful.

The other caution is about reproductions. The more popular black collectibles become, the more people will reproduce them. Some of these reproductions are well marked and clearly new. Others are less so, and have been known to fool even experienced collectors. Again, exercise great care and ask questions. When in doubt, "just say no!"

The lefthand number is the page number. The letters following it indicate the position of the photograph on the page: T=top, L=left, TL=top left, TR=top right, C=center, CL=center left, CR=center right, R=right, B=bottom, BL=bottom left, BR=bottom right. In photos with more that one object, they are identified. The right hand numbers are the estimated price ranges. N/A signifies either that a value was not reliably available or that the contributor did not wish to have the value included in this guide.

Page	Position	Value
1		N/A
2		N/A
3		$350-400
5		45-55
6		Very rare
7		45-55
8		Rare
9		N/A
10		45-50
11		385-425
12		250-275
13		850-950
14	TL	2500-3500
	TR	Rare
	BL	350-400
	BC	2500-3000
	BR	2500-3250
15	TR	N/A
	BL	N/A
	BR	N/A
16	TL	N/A
	BL	450-600
	BR	450-600
17	TL	675-800
	TR	850-925
	BL	If mint 950-1000
	BR	850-950
18	TL	1100-1200
	TR	900-1050
	CL	700-800
	BL	1000-1100
	BR	900-1000
19	TL	900-1050
	TR	N/A
	BL	150-200
	BR	150-200

Page	Position	Value
20	T	N/A
	BL	N/A
	BR	N/A
21	TL	50-125
	TR	150-200
	BL	45-60
	BR	400-600
22	TL	4500-6000
	TR	N/A
	BL	Each 45-60
	BR	500-600
23		N/A
24		N/A
25		N/A
26		N/A
27		N/A
28		N/A
29		N/A
30		N/A
32	TL	N/A
	TR	N/A
	BL	300-400
	BR	N/A
33	T	Set 500
	BL	125-150
	BR	65-80
34	T	Each 35-50
	B	85-100
35	TL	N/A
	TR	Rare
	BL	N/A
36	TL	300-375
	TR	N/A
	BL	300-375
	BR	Pair 225-250
37	TL	350-450

Page	Position	Value
	TC	N/A
	TR	N/A
	B	N/A
38	TL	N/A
	TR	N/A
	B	650 and up
39	TL	175-300
	TC	100-150
	TR	N/A
	BL	150-200
	BR	125-150
40		N/A
41	TL	N/A
	TR	125-150
	BL	85-100
42		N/A
43		N/A
44	TL	N/A
	TR	N/A
	BL	N/A
	BR	500-600
45		N/A
46	T	250-350
	BL	250-350
	BR	175-225
47		N/A
48	TL	N/A
	TR	N/A
	BL	N/A
	BR	150-200
49	T	N/A
	B	45-60
50	TL	45-60
	TR	35-40
	BL	N/A
	BR	If mint $145-160

Page	Position	Value
51	T	N/A
	BL	1200-1400
	BR	1200-1400
52	TL	165-185
	TR	125-140
	BL	85-100
	BR	l: 125-140 r: 450-525
53	TL	165-200
	TR	N/A
	BL	N/A
	BR	1200-1400
54	L	N/A
	TR	375-450
	BR	N/A
55	BR	20-25
56	TL	30-40
	TR	20-25
57	TL	20-25
	TR	15-20
58	TL	20-25
	TC	20-25
	TR	15-20
	BL	20-25
	BR	15-20
59	TL	30-40
	TR	25-30
	BL	30-40
	BR	20-25
60	T	40-45
	BL	125-140
	BR	35-40
61	T	45-60
	BL	60-85
	BR	25-30
62	TL	30-35

Ceramic salt and pepper shakers in the shape of a child's head and a slice of watermelon. *Courtesy of Jan Lindenberger, Black By Popular Demand, Colorado Springs, Colorado.*

Ceramic salt and pepper shakers with 22k gold trim. *Courtesy of Jan Lindenberger, Black By Popular Demand, Colorado Springs, Colorado.*

Japanese ceramic salt and pepper shakers, 3" high. *Courtesy of Jan Lindenberger, Black By Popular Demand, Colorado Springs, Colorado.*

Three inch high Japanese-made ceramic salt and pepper shakers. *Courtesy of Jan Lindenberger, Black By Popular Demand, Colorado Springs, Colorado.*

Other Kitchen Items

Metal copy of recipe box with plaster face, manufactured by F & F Mold & Die Company. 4" x 5". *Courtesy of Jan Lindenberger, Black By Popular Demand, Colorado Springs, Colorado.*

Little Black Sambo syrup pitcher from the Sambo Restaurant chain. Glass, plastic, and metal, 11″ tall. *Courtesy of Jan Lindenberger, Black By Popular Demand, Colorado Springs, Colorado.*

Wooden knife holder with plaster face, 9″ tall. *Courtesy of Jan Lindenberger, Black By Popular Demand, Colorado Springs, Colorado.*

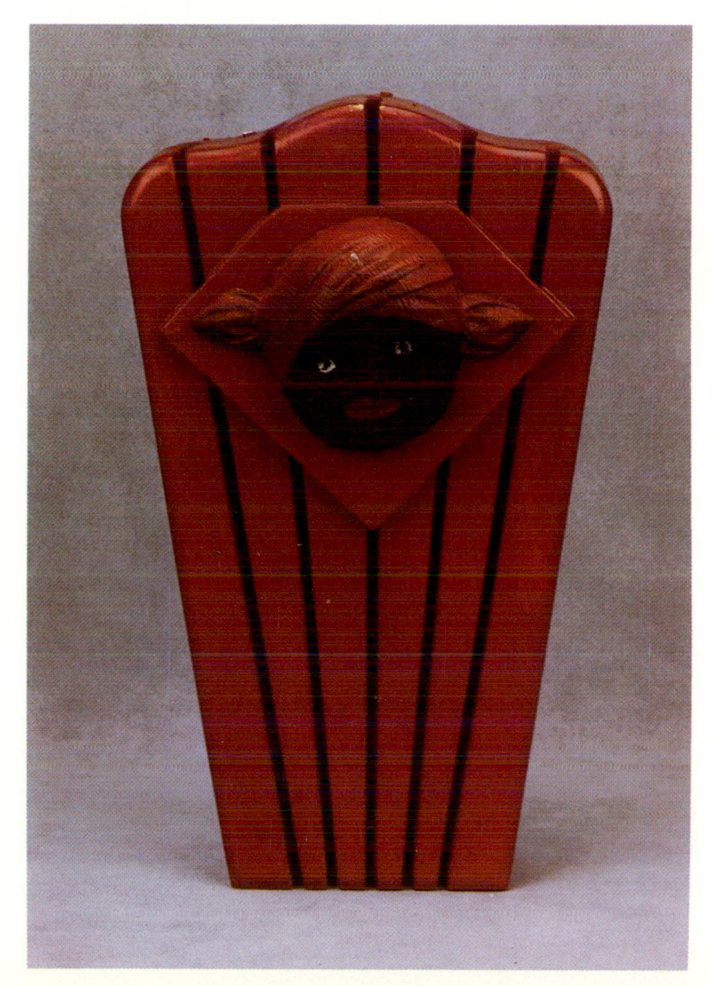

Aunt Jemima syrup pitcher of molded plastic, manufactured by the F & F Mold & Die Company, Dayton, Ohio, 1950s. 5.5″ high. *Courtesy of Jan Lindenberger, Black By Popular Demand, Colorado Springs, Colorado.*

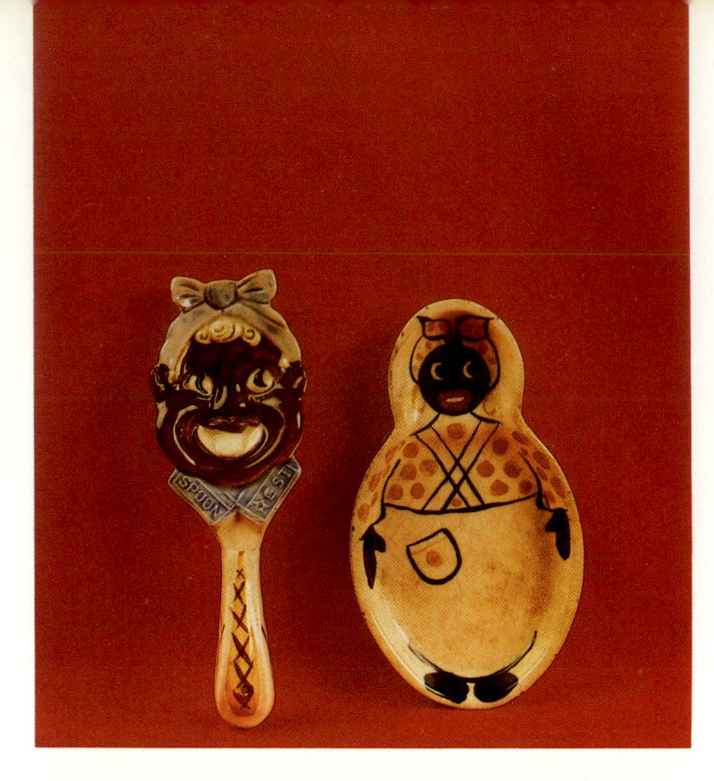

Ceramic spoon rests. 6.5″ long. *Courtesy of Jan Lindenberger, Black By Popular Demand, Colorado Springs, Colorado.*

Ceramic egg timer. *Courtesy of Jan Lindenberger, Black By Popular Demand, Colorado Springs, Colorado.*

Painted wood match holder. 14″ tall. *Courtesy of Bunny Walker.*

Wobbly jaw bisque match holder. 4″ high. *Courtesy of John Haley, Halifax, England.*

Bisque chef's head string holder. 8″ tall. *Courtesy of Jan Lindenberger, Black By Popular Demand, Colorado Springs, Colorado.*

Ceramic dinner bell, 1989. *Courtesy of Jan Lindenberger, Black By Popular Demand, Colorado Springs, Colorado.*

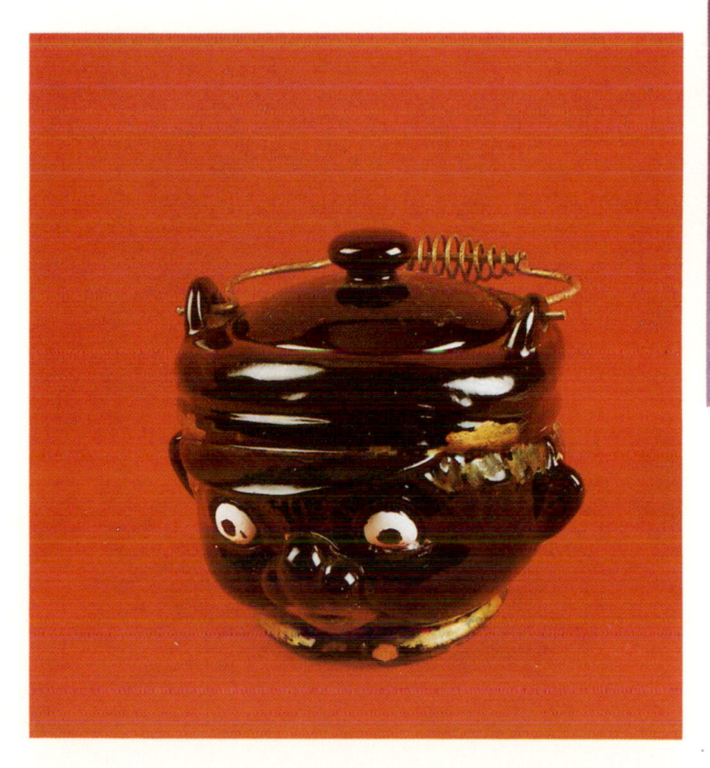

This ceramic sugar bowl with metal handle has a matching tea pot and creamer. 5″ high. *Courtesy of Jan Lindenberger, Black By Popular Demand, Colorado Springs, Colorado.*

Kitchen towels, linen with needlework and applique. *Courtesy of Elizabeth Holt and Scott Lofquist.*

Three potholders. *Courtesy of Elizabeth Holt and Scott Lofquist.*

Printed linen towel. *Courtesy of Elizabeth Holt and Scott Lofquist.*

Miscellaneous Household Goods

No. 123 Mammy Memo and pencil holder. Plastic, 10.5" tall. *Courtesy of Bunny Walker.*

Printed linen guest towel, copyright 1952 by Nell Fulton. *Courtesy of Holt's Country Store, Grandview, Missouri.*

Hanging laundry bag with needle work and applique. *Courtesy of Elizabeth Holt and Scott Lofquist.*

Printed cotton guest towel with applied ribbons, contemporary. *Courtesy of Holt's Country Store, Grandview, Missouri.*

"By Gum! Him Turban Afire!" soft paste mug with transfer decoration, nineteenth century. *Courtesy of a private collection.*

"Rule of Three" soft paste mug with transfer decoration, nineteenth century. *Courtesy of a private collection.*

Coon Chicken Inn dinner plate. *Courtesy of Holt's Country Store, Grandview, Missouri.*

Lithographed child's playset with matching tin cup and plate of black children, nineteenth century. *Courtesy of Holt's Country Store, Grandview, Missouri.*

Tin pail of a similar design as the preceding cup and bowl, also with a transfer picture, 1910-1915. 3″ high. *Courtesy of Jan Lindenberger, Black By Popular Demand, Colorado Springs, Colorado.*

Porcelain pitcher with painted picture of black man. *Courtesy of a private collection.*

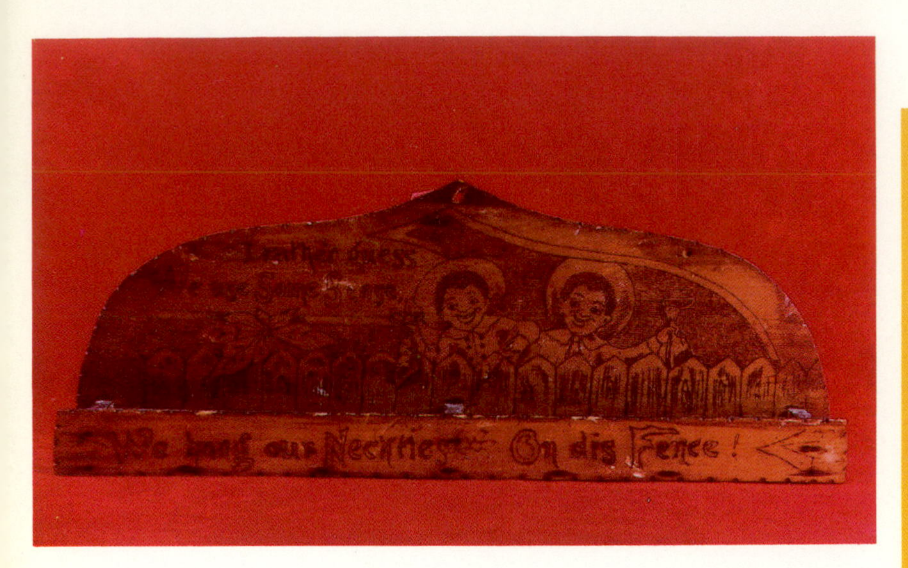

Wooden tie rack by Flemish Art. 6″ x 16″. *Courtesy of Jan Lindenberger, Black By Popular Demand, Colorado Springs, Colorado.*

Bakelite sailor pin. *Courtesy of Dee Battle.*

Black eraser protector. *Courtesy of Holt's Country Store, Grandview, Missouri.*

Clothes brush, painted wood and bristle. 8.5″. *Courtesy of Jan Lindenberger, Black By Popular Demand, Colorado Springs, Colorado.*

Left: pin with eyes that move when the string is pulled; right: comic pin. *Courtesy of Elizabeth Holt and Scott Lofquist.*

A rare American cast iron nut cracker, ca. 1870s. 8″ high. *Courtesy of Frank G. Whitson, Baltimore, Maryland.*

Left: a decorative pin; right: a bottle opener. *Courtesy of Sweeney's Spot.*

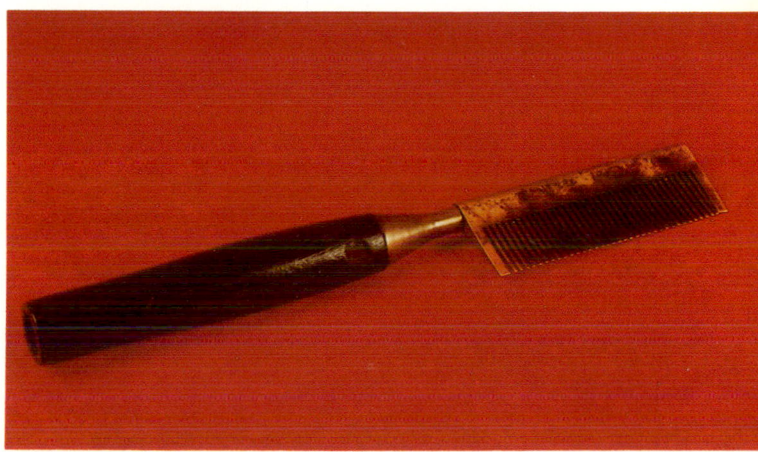

Lock straightener similar to Madam C.J. Walker's Steel Comb. *Courtesy of Jan Lindenberger, Black By Popular Demand, Colorado Springs, Colorado.*

Beautiful and unique hooked rugs. *Courtesy of Harry W. and Barbara C. Hepburn, Harrison, Maine.*

Celluloid retractable tape measure. German, ca. 1920. 1" high. *Courtesy of Stuart Cropper, Sussex, England.*

Lead pencil sharpener. German, 1920s. 2" high. *Courtesy of John Haley, Halifax, England.*

Plastic alligator pencil holder with pencil and black head. *Courtesy of a private collection.*

Clocks and Watches

Two wind-up table clocks. 3.5″ tall. *Courtesy of Neat Olde Things, Stewartsville, New Jersey.*

Automaton table clock. The shoeshine boy moves his arm up and down. The Lux Clock Mfg. Co., Waterbury, Connecticut. *Courtesy of a private collection.*

Little Black Sambo clock with subsidiary second hand. Winding movement, ca. 1946. Made in the U.S. *Courtesy of Neat Olde Things, Stewartsville, New Jersey.*

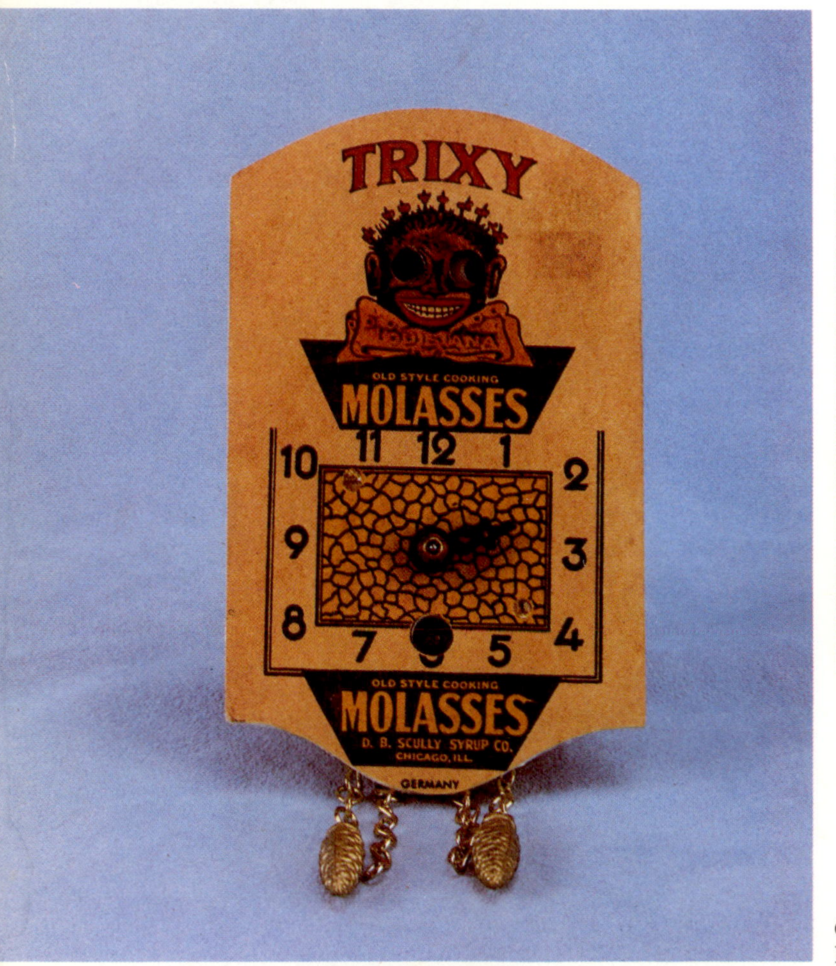

A German clock advertising Trixy Old Style Cooking Molasses, D.B. Scully Syrup Co., Chicago, Ill. The face is plywood and the eyes move back and forth. *Courtesy of Neat Olde Things, Stewartsville, New Jersey.*

Tin toy pocket watch with paper dial. *Courtesy of a private collection.*

Opposite page:
Mechanical bank marked England. Similar to Steven's "Jolly Nigger," he has a lever behind his left shoulder which raises his hand to his mouth, depositing a coin. The eyes roll down when the lever is pushed. Painted cast iron, 6" x 5". *Courtesy of Margaret B. Schiffer.*

A Note to Collectors

From the preceding pages the variety of black collectibles should be clear. While it is possible to be a general collector of black memorabilia, many have chosen to specialize in a particular form. The old adage of collectors holds true: "Collect what you like!"

Of course, even the purest of collectors is concerned with the value of their collection. The beginning collector should develop an eye for quality and rarity. These two factors are the strongest in determining the long term investment value of an item. While one may adopt a strategy of entering the market at the lower end, the finer, less plentiful pieces might well be worth the sacrifice.

Whatever strategy you choose, seek the advice of an experienced collector or dealer. With the growing popularity of the black collectibles, copies and fakes have become a problem to collectors. Some of these items are so well rendered that even the experienced veteran has been fooled. Check the authenticity of an item before making your investment. A good dealer will welcome your inquiries and be more than willing to provide you with the information you seek. If there are questions about a particular piece, leave it for someone else.

Collecting these images in black is an interesting, educational, challenging, and sometimes frustrating endeavor. Be careful as you go and have fun along the way.

"Jerry's Smile", Tin advertising tray, M.K. Goetz Brewing Co., St. Joseph, Missouri. *Courtesy of Betty and R.C. Hursman.*

"Old Kentucky Home," dancing figures in a wooden box, ca. 1870. *Schneider's Antique Toys, Lancaster, Pennsylvania.*

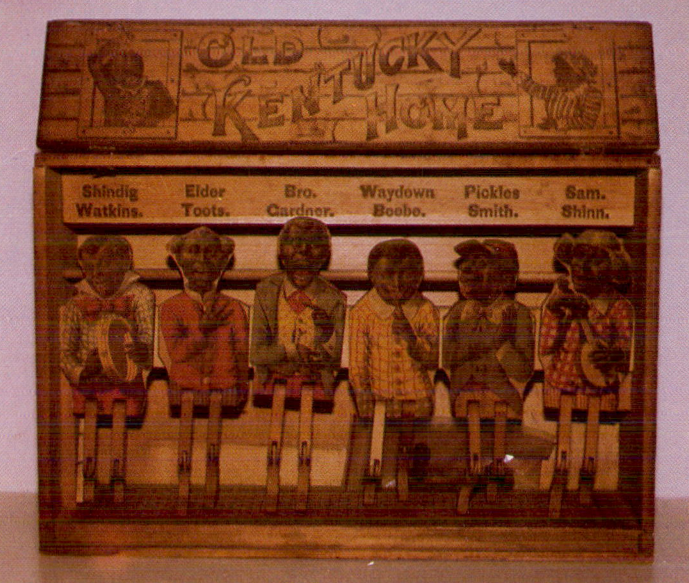

Bibliography

"The Stump Speaker" mechanical bank named after a popular minstrelsy routine.

Angione, Genevieve. *All-Bisque & Half-Bisque Dolls.* West Chester, Pennsylvania: Schiffer Publishing Ltd., 1981.

Cieslik, Jürgen & Marianne. *Lehman Toys, The History of E.P. Lehmann—1881-1981.* Münich: New Cavendish Books, 1982.

Devisse, Jean. *The Image of the Black in Western Art, Volume II, Part 1.* Cambridge, Massachusetts: Harvard University Press, 1979.

Ellison, Ralph. *Invisible Man.* New York: New American Library, 1952.

Ethnic Images in Advertising, a catalogue for an exhibition of the same name. Philadelphia: The Balch Institute for Ethnic Studies, 1984.

Franklin, John Hope. *From Slavery to Freedom: A History of Negro Americans.* New York: Alfred A. Knopf, 1967.

Gibbs, P.J. *Black Collectibles: Sold in America.* Paducah, Kentucky: Collector Books, 1987.

Gossett, Thomas F. *Race: The History of an Idea in America.* New York: Schocken Books, 1963.

Haynes, Robert V., Editor. *Blacks in White America Before 1865.* New York: David McKay Company, Inc., 1972.

Jones, LeRoi. *Blues People: Negro Music in White America.* New York: William Morrow and Company, 1963.

Locke, Alain. *The Negro in Art: A Pictorial Record of the Negro Artist and of the Negro Theme in Art.* New York: Hacker Art Books, 1968.

McElroy, Guy C. *Facing History: The Black Image in American Art 1710-1940.* San Francisco: Bedford Arts, Publishers, in association with The Corcoran Gallery of Art, 1990.

Nelson, Pamela B. *Ethnic Images in Toys and Games.* Philadelphia: The Balch Institute for Ethnic Studies, 1990.

Parry, Ellwood. *The Image of the Indian and the Black Man in American Art, 1590-1900.* New York: George Braziller, 1974.

Quarles, Benjamin. *The Negro in the Making of America.* New York: Collier Books, 1964.

Reno, Dawn E. *Collecting Black Americana.* New York: Crown Publishers Inc., 1986.

Smith, Darrell A. *Black Americana: A Personal Collection.* Minneapolis: Star Press, 1988.

Toll, Robert C. *Blacking Up: The Minstrel Show in Nineteenth-Century America.* New York: Oxford University Press, 1974.

Twombly, Robert C. *Blacks in White America Since 1865.* New York: David McKay Company, Inc., 1971.

Whitton, Blair. *American Clockwork Toys, 1862-1900.* West Chester, Pennsylvania: Schiffer Publishing, 1981.

Woodward, C. Vann. *The Strange Career of Jim Crow.* New York: Oxford University Press, 1966.

Young, Jackie. *Black Collectibles: Mammy and her friends.* West Chester, Pennsylvania: Schiffer Publishing Ltd., 1988.